Shakespeare Scenes

Monologues for young adult female actors

Compiled & edited by

Kim Gilbert

DEDICATION

This collection of Shakespearean scenes, is dedicated to all students of drama and those readers with a love of the greatest writer to have ever lived – William Shakespeare. Continue to explore his works. I hope you gain as much satisfaction from them as I have.

ACKNOWLEDGEMENTS

A special thanks goes to my husband Steve, who has prepared this collection for publication, and has bailed me out on numerous occasions over the years, with his technical expertise.

Contents

INTRODUCTION

I have personally compiled and edited this collection of Shakespearean scenes specifically for aspiring female actors to study as well as enjoy. The scenes within this book are most suited to older, teenage actors, who have already begun to acquire some of the technical skills necessary to perform Shakespeare's wonderfully drawn, young adult female characters. These scenes are suitable for a range of acting exams and awards as well as for auditions and festivals. I have tried and tested these scenes with numerous students over the years with great success and more importantly, they have thoroughly enjoyed working on them. I have not provided guidelines as to how to perform these scenes. This is something for the individual performer to explore and what is what will make your performance individual. However, I do strongly believe, it is crucial to play characters within ones' playing range. As a developing actor, in your late teens and beyond, now is the time to tackle the more demanding female characters which Shakespeare has so brilliantly created. Continue to build your vocal skills and acting technique systematically: in this way your performances will have the necessary depth and will be exciting to watch. Learn to discover your characters subtext and objectives. This will enable your characters to spring to life and hence help your audience believe in you. Methodical preparation will pay dividends when exploring these fascinating characters. I hope you enjoy working on them!

WILLIAM SHAKESPEARE 1564-1616

Shakespeare was born in Stratford-on-Avon. It is thought that he went to the Grammar School even though there are no records to prove this. His parents were both illiterate. William certainly went on to make a name for himself and the surname of Shakespeare, despite being quite common in those days, became famous. William Shakespeare's legacy was his 37 world renowned plays as well as his 154 sonnets

Shakespeare married Anne Hathaway, she was 8yrs older than William; the couple had 3 children by the time he was 21, Susanna and twins Judith and Hamnet. Shakespeare finally left Stratford for London to seek his fortune, possibly at the age of around 23yrs. It is thought that the 'Queen's Men' visited Stratford to perform and William joined them as a young recruit. Shakespeare's first London patron was James Burbage, a leading theatrical manager of the time. Later, his son Richard Burbage would play many of Shakespeare's leading roles. Many of the leading playwrights of the day were jealous of Shakespeare and they mocked him for not having been to University. By the age of twenty-eight, Shakespeare was well established in London as an actor and playwright. Richard Burbage later formed a new troupe called the Lord Chamberlain's Men, of which Shakespeare was a member and remained so until the end of his career. Burbage's carpenters built the highly successful Globe Theatre in 1599 with a capacity of 2,500- 3,000. The original Globe Theatre in London was known as 'The Wooden 'O' because of its shape. Shakespeare owned a tenth of this theatre. Shakespeare wrote a range of plays loosely categorized as tragedies, comedies and histories. Shakespeare based the plots of his plays on traditional stories, often changing them slightly or adding music and songs to make them more interesting. Superstition was as important as religion in Elizabethan times. That is why so many of Shakespeare's plays feature ghosts, witches, spells, magic, fairies and storms and shipwrecks.

It certainly helped that Queen Elizabeth 1 loved the theatre and invited players to entertain at Court. There were no female actresses, only male actors. The young boys played the women's parts. Many of the audience had to stand to watch the plays and were known as groundlings. There were, of course, seats and shelter available at a higher price for the wealthier. If an Elizabethan audience didn't like a play, they often booed and jeered, cracked nuts and threw orange skins.

The actors were given only their own parts to the play. It wasn't until the 16th and 17th Century that printing became available, enabling Shakespeare's plays to be published. However, printers would often change the words of a playwrights play in order for them to fit onto the page!

Unfortunately, it was due to The Great Plague in 1665 that all London theatres were closed down, forcing players to tour the rest of the country.

Shakespeare's characters and plots

Shakespeare's characters are depicted as real people with 'universal' emotions. His variety of characters interrelate with other characters creating great interest within the plot. His comedies often include stock- characters, which are easily recognizable characters with common features and characteristics.

Acting a Shakespearean Character

When preparing for acting a role one should always study the play as a whole and approach the scene in context with the whole play.

Here are some questions to consider.

Is your character a central character i.e. the hero or heroine providing strength and leadership, or perhaps a stock character providing comedy or light relief to the plot?

What are your character's likes, dislikes?

Map your character's journey throughout the play?

How does your character develop throughout the play?

What is your character's role/purpose in the play? Try to establish their objective.

Is your character a central character (i.e. hero/heroine) or a stock character (comedy or lowly small part character)?

Does this character suit your acting skills and personality?

Think about how you might like to play your character in terms of physical and vocal skills?

What characteristics would the actor need to play this character?

How do you relate to your character? Do you like your character?

How do you envisage your character in costume?

Shakespeare's Writing style

Metre and Rhythm

English is a stress language. This means that our language is made up of strong and weak stresses. Verse is made of these stresses into regular patterns which is what we call METRE.

A metrical unit is called a FOOT. This comes from ancient Greece, where, in dance, the foot was raised up and down on the beat of a bar of music.

A metrical line is named according to the number of feet in a line.

IAMBIC

Iambic has one unstressed & one stressed syllable OR one weak syllable & one strong syllable. **Iambic Pentametre** (used by Shakespeare & other writers) is made up of 5 feet of iambic rhythms e.g. de dum/de dum/de dum/de dum/de dum. e.g. 'The clock struck nine when I did send the nurse' and 'I left no ring with her, what means this lady?'

The rhythm resembles the beating of the human heart and is closest to the natural rhythm of natural speech. Blank verse is the closest rhythm to natural speech.

Shakespeare wrote in **iambic pentametre** or **blank verse (verse without rhyme).** It has no regular rhyme and is therefore ideal for writing verse plays. There are, however, inversions and other variations which are added to create variety in the rhythm. Shakespeare often uses prose writing to vary his writing too. This is often reserved to the lower status characters, but not always. Be aware of the hemistich: where one character speaks half a line and the next character finishes it. This is where you may see split or half lines on a page between two characters speaking.

Shakespeare's Language

Here are some of Shakespeare's famous expressions which we still use today. Shakespeare's plays were full of insults and rude words. Some of these words were highly insulting and seem very amusing to present day audiences.

There's method in my madness: The world's your oyster: Love is blind:

beetle-head: pottle-deep: pribbling: flap-mouthed: fat-kidneyed: wart-necked:

swag-bellied: onion-eyed: bum-bailey: maggot-pie: pignut.

To name but a few!

The Scenes

MUCH ADO ABOUT NOTHING

Much ado about nothing is a comedy. The themes are courtship and marriage. The governor of Messina in Sicily, is awaiting the arrival of the Prince of Arragon and two lords, Benedick and Claudio. They have been invited to spend a month at the palace. There are two young heroines; one is the governor's niece, Beatrice and the other, Hero. Beatrice and Benedick enjoy a witty love/hate relationship. Meanwhile, Claudio has fallen in love with Hero and the Governor, approving of this match, holds a masked ball in their honor. Many wish Beatrice and Benedick to be married as they feel they are well suited. However, both are averse to marriage. The prince has a wicked brother, Don Juan, who tries to disrupt these friendships. He tells Claudio that the Prince is in love with Hero. He orchestrates a scene to appear that Hero has been unfaithful to Claudio. Later, these misdemeanors are discovered. Benedick's is persuaded by his friends that he should marry. A plan to join these reluctant lovers is underway. Two comic constables, Dogberry and Verges, are left in charge of overseeing the marriage arrangements of Hero and Claudio. Two watchmen discover Don Juan's plot but unfortunately, the Prince is too busy to listen to this discovery and the wedding takes place. However, Claudio halts the ceremony by refusing to marry Hero as he believes the story of her infidelity. Everyone sides with Claudio except for the Friar, Benedick and Beatrice. Hero faints as a result of this and people are led to believe that she is dead. Hero's father believes his daughter is innocent and challenges Claudio to a duel. Thankfully, the plot to blacken Hero's name is revealed and the perpetrators confess their crime. Claudio is now distraught, believing Hero to be dead. Hero's father arranges for him to marry another lady who looks just like his daughter. A double wedding is quickly arranged between Claudio and Hero and Beatrice and Benedick. It is at this point that Claudio realizes his bride is, in fact, his beloved Hero.

MUCH ADO ABOUT NOTHING ACT 2, SC 1

(Beatrice is talking to Leonato & Antonio. Beatrice is discussing the attributes of a perfect man; a combination of Don Juan and Benedick (one talks too much, the other too little). Beatrice believes she will never find a husband who meets her demanding criteria).

Beatrice:

How tartly that gentleman looks! I never can see him but I am heart-burned an hour after.

He were an excellent man that were made just in the mid-way between him and Benedick: the one is too like an image, and says nothing; and the other too like my lady's eldest son, evermore tattling.

With a good leg and a good foot, uncle, and money enough in his purse, such a man would win any woman in the world, if he could get her good will.

Too curst is more than curst: I shall lessen God's sending that way; for it is said, 'God sends a curst cow short horns': but to a cow too curst he sends none. Just, if he send me no husband; for the which blessing I am at him upon my knees every morning and evening. Lord! I could not endure a husband with a beard on his face; I had rather lie in the woolen!

A husband with no beard, what should I do with him? Dress him in my apparel and make him my waiting-gentle-woman? He that hath a beard is more than a youth, and he that hath no beard is less than a man; and he that is more than a youth is not for me; and he that is less than a man, I am not for him: therefore, I will even take sixpence in earnest of the bear-ward, and lead his apes into hell.

But no, I go not into hell but to the gate; and there will the devil meet me, like an old cuckold, with horns on his head, and say,

'Get you to heaven, Beatrice, get you to heaven; here's no place for you maids'. So, deliver I up my apes, and away to Saint Peter: the heavens, he shows me where the bachelors sit, and there live we as merry as the day is long.

Yes faith, it is my cousin's duty to make curtsy, and say, 'Father, as it please you'. But yet for all that, cousin, let him be a handsome fellow, or else make another curtsy, and say, 'Father, as it please me.'

Not till God make men of some other mettle than earth. Would it not grieve a woman to be overmastered with a piece of valiant dust? to make an account of her life to a clod of wayward marl? No, uncle, I'll none: Adam's sons are my brethren, and truly I hold it a sin to match in my kindred.

The fault will be in the music, cousin, if you be not wooed in good time: if the prince be too important, tell him there is measure in everything, and so dance out the answer; For hear me, Hero - wooing, wedding, and repenting, as a Scotch jig, a measure and a cinque-pace: the first suit is hot and hasty like a Scotch jig, and full as fantastical; the wedding mannerly-modest, as a measure, full of state and ancientry; and then comes Repentance, and with his bad legs falls into the cinque-pace faster and faster, till he sink into his grave.

I have a good eye, uncle - I can see a church by daylight.

MUCH ADO ABOUT NOTHING ACT 3, SC 1

(Leonato's garden. Hero is with her ladies in waiting, Margaret and Ursula. They are planning to trick Beatrice into realizing her love for Benedick).

Hero:

Good Margaret, run thee to the parlor;

There shall thou find my cousin Beatrice

Proposing with the prince and Claudio:

Whisper her ear and tell her, I and Ursula

Walk in the orchard and our whole discourse

Is all of her; say that thou overheard'st us;

And bid her steal into the pleached bower,

Where honeysuckles, ripen'd by the sun,

Forbid the sun to enter, like favourites,

Made proud by princes, that advance their pride

Against that power that bred it: there will she hide her,

To listen our purpose. This is thy office;

Bear thee well in it and leave us alone.

Now, Ursula, when Beatrice doth come,

As we do trace this alley up and down,

Our talk must only be of Benedick.

When I do name him, let it be thy part

To praise him more than ever man did merit:

My talk must only be of Benedick.

My talk to thee must be how Benedick

Is sick in love with Beatrice. Of this matter

Is little Cupid's crafty arrow made,

That only wounds by hearsay.

(Beatrice enters)

Now begin;

For look where Beatrice, like a lapwing, runs

Close by the ground, to hear our conference.

Then go we near her, that her ear lose nothing

Of the false sweet bait that we lay for it.

(Hero is fully aware that Beatrice is listening).

No, truly, Ursula, she is too disdainful;

I know her spirits are as coy and wild

As haggards of the rock.

So says the prince and my new-trothed lord.

They did entreat me to acquaint her of it;

But I persuaded them, if they loved Benedick,

To wish him wrestle with affection,

And never to let Beatrice know of it.

O God of Love! I know he doth deserve

As much as may be yielded to a man:

But Nature never framed a woman's heart

Of prouder stuff than that of Beatrice;

Disdain and scorn ride sparkling in her eyes,

Misprising what they look on, and her wit

Values itself so highly that to her

All matter else seems weak: she cannot love,

Nor take no shape nor project of affection.

She is so self-endeared.

ALL'S WELL THAT ENDS WELL

The play starts with the Countess of Rousillon sending her son, Bertram to the French court to visit the King who is seriously ill. A young, gentle woman named Helena, the daughter of a doctor, is in love with Bertram, although as she is of much lower status, there is no chance of them marrying. The Countess is nevertheless extremely fond of Helena and knows that she is in love with her son. There is another soldier named Parolles who is less than trustworthy. Bertram is unaware of his true nature and befriends him. Parolles goes to the Court and later to Italy with Bertram. When Helena suggests she may have a remedy to help the ailing king, the Countess suggests she go to the French court in order to assist the King with her knowledge of medicine. At first, the King refuses to see any doctor but Helena insists that she can cure him. Finally, the King agrees to allow Helena to treat him, stating that if she can cure him, she will be entitled to marry any man of her choosing. Helena miraculously cures the king unlike any other doctor has been able to do before and without hesitation, she chooses Bertram to be her husband. However, Bertram believes Helena is too lowly in status and refuses to marry her. The King kindly offers to raise Helena's status so that they are equals but Bertram still refuses her hand as he is not in love with her. The King insists that they marry anyway even though Helena tries to release him from this agreement. Bertram tells Helena that until she can get the ring upon his finger, they will never be truly married. He is confident that he has tricked her.

Meanwhile, abroad, there are wars in Italy and so, keen to participate in the fighting as well as escape his marriage to Helena, Bertram flees shortly after the marriage ceremony. The Countess, having approved of the marriage, is furious with her son. Helena, distraught by all that has happened, leaves Bertram a letter to say that she herself will leave the Court, leaving Bertram free to return to France and spare him the dangers of war. Helena then goes on a pilgrimage. In Italy, despite Bertram being a brave soldier and earning honours for himself, he is also a womaniser and has been trying to woo a young Florentine girl named Diana. Coincidentally, Helena visits Florence as part of her pilgrimage and befriends Diana and her mother. On hearing that Bertram is in fact already married, Diana wishes he would return to his wife. A plot is hatched between the women for Diana to surrender to Bertram in exchange for his ring: the ring which belongs to Helena. On refusing at first to hand over the ring, Bertram eventually agrees as he is desperate to sleep with Diana. Diana says she will also give him a ring in exchange. The plot is set and as it is night time, Bertram does not realize that he has in fact spent the night with his own wife, Helena.

Time passes and Bertram is led to believe that Helena is now dead. He returns to Rousillon where the Countess is also mourning Helena. When the King arrives, he is willing to forgive Bertram until he sees the ring on Bertram's finger. He recognized the ring which had belonged to Helena. Diana arrives and tells everyone about what had happened between herself and Bertram which infuriates the King further until Helena enters and reveals all. Bertram is wearing Helena's ring and she can now truly be his wife. Bertram happily accepts this. Helena has won the wager. The Countess is delighted to have Helena as her daughter in law and the King gives her a large dowry. The play can loosely be described as a comedy as it has a happy ending.

ALL'S WELL THAT ENDS WELL ACT 3, SC 2

(The lowly gentlewomen, Helena has been allowed to marry Bertram, as a favour for having cured the King of his illness. Unfortunately, Bertram does not love Helena and has fled France, vowing never to return until the marriage has been dissolved. Bertram has left Helena a letter).

Helena:

"Till I have no wife I have nothing in France".

Nothing in France until he has no wife!

Thou shalt have none, Rousillon, none in France;

Then hast thou all again. Poor lord, is't I

That chase thee from thy country and expose

Those tender limbs of thine to the event

Of the none-sparing war? And is it I

That drive thee from the sportive court, where thou

Was't shot at with fair eyes, to be the mark

Of smoky muskets? O you leaden messengers

That ride upon the violent speed of fire,

Fly with false aim, cleave the still-piecing air

That sings with piercing, do not touch my lord.

Whoever shoots at him, I set him there.

Whoever charges on his forward breast,

I am the caitiff that do hold him to't,

And though I kill him not, I am the cause

His death was so effected. Better 'twere

I met the ravin' lion when he roared

With sharp constraint of hunger; better 'twere

That all the miseries which nature owes

Were mine at once. No, come thou home, Rousillon,

Whence honor but of danger wins a scar,

As oft it loses all. I will be gone;

My being here it is that holds thee hence.

Shall I stay here to do't? No, no, although

The air of paradise did fan the house

And angels officed all. I will be gone,

That pitiful rumor may report my flight

To consulate thine ear. Come night, end day!

For with the dark, poor thief, I'll steal away

THE TAMING OF THE SHREW

This comedy is set in Padua, Italy. Baptista, a wealthy merchant has two daughters, Katharina and Bianca. Katharina is the eldest whom no one wants to marry because she is so bad-tempered. Her younger sister, Bianca, is the opposite and is gentle and amiable. Bianca has two marriage proposals, one young suitor and an older suitor, but her father vows that she will not be able marry either of them until he has found a suitable marriage partner for his eldest daughter, Katharina.

A young visitor to the area, Lucentio, overhears the town's gossip, and on seeing the kindly Bianca, falls in love with her. In order to get closer to her, he swaps places with his servant, in order to become Bianca's teacher. Another man called Petruchio has also arrived in Padua, with his servant Grumio, in search of a rich wife. In fact, there are several suitors who visit Baptista's house to woo Bianca. All are desperate for Katharina to find someone who will marry her. Petruchio and Katharina are a strong match for each other. Both are highly spirited and stubborn. Petruchio takes on the challenge to woo Katharina. He offers to marry her and in order to tame her, he teases Katharina ruthlessly. Bianca's four suitors are relieved at Petruchio's marriage proposal as they are now in a position to ask for Bianca's hand. The two wealthy suitors offer huge sums of money to Baptista, whilst the two less wealthy suitors, attempt to woo her with music, poetry and love.

The wedding preparations for Katharina and Petruchio begin. The wedding is a complete fiasco. Petruchio is unsuitably dressed and late for the ceremony. His behavior is unruly and before the celebrations are over, he whisks Katherina away to his country house, where his servants are waiting for them. He treats her with such little respect. His aim is to tame the shrew she is reputed to be. He practically starves poor Katharina into submission and teases her with fine new clothes which he then refuses to give her.

Meanwhile, back in Padua, Bianca has fallen in love with Lucentio. The other suitors now need to be dismissed. Luciento's servant finds a street beggar to pretend to be Luciento's father to give permission for the couple to wed. Luciento plans to run away and conduct a secret wedding with Bianca. However, Luciento's real father, Vincentio, is unexpectedly journeying to Padua. On his way there, he bumps into Petruchio and Katharina. Petruchio is still insisting he is in charge of the relationship and Katharina has to agree with everything he says. There is much comedy to be enjoyed. When Vincentio arrives in Padua he discovers that his son is not his son at all but his servant in disguise. Lucentio then returns with his new bride, Bianca, and begs his father for forgiveness. There is a large banquet in honour of the two newly married couples: Katharina and Petruchio and Bianca and Luciento. During the banquet, courtiers offer their sympathies to Petruchio for having such a disobedient wife. Petruchio says that on the contrary he now has the most obedient wife of all. In fact, he lays a bet with them about this. When the other two men summon their wives, they do not come whereas when Petruchio orders Katharina to his side, she swiftly obeys exclaiming that she is a changed woman and now an obedient wife.

THE TAMING OF THE SHREW ACT 5, SC 3

(Katharina is now married to Petruchio and he is starving her, in order for her to learn the error of her ways. He is hoping she will succumb into being a dutiful wife).

Katharina:

The more my wrong, the more his spite appears.

What, did he marry me to famish me?

Beggars, that come unto my father's door,

Upon entreaty, have a present alms;

If not, elsewhere they meet with charity:

But I, who never knew how to entreat,

Nor never needed that I should entreat,

Am starv'd for meat, giddy for lack of sleep;

With oaths kept waking, and with brawling fed.

And that which spites me more than all these wants,

He does it under name of perfect love;

As who should say, if I should sleep, or eat,

'Twere deadly sickness, or else present death.

I pr'ythee go, and get me some repast;

(She is asked what she would like to eat)

I care not what, so it be wholesome food.

To a neat's foot?

'T is passing good: I pr'ythee let me have it.

(Katharina is teased with an array of food which she is not allowed to eat)

I like it well: good Grumio, fetch it me.

Why, then the beef, and let the mustard rest.

Then both, or one, or anything thou wilt.

(By this time, she is so enraged that she has not been allowed to eat any of the food which has been offered to her. She is ravenous)

Go, get thee gone, thou false deluding slave.

That feed'st me with the very name of meat.

Sorrow on thee, and all the pack of you,

That triumph thus upon my misery!

Go, get thee gone, I say.

THE TAMING OF THE SHREW ACT 5, SC 3

(Katherina has finally learned the duties of a good wife – or has she? This is the final speech of the play and Katharina is asked by Petruchio to offer advice to her fellow headstrong women as to their duties as wives).

Katharina:

Fie, fie! Unknit that threatening unkind brow,

And dart not scornful glances from those eyes,

To wound thy lord, thy king, thy governor:

It blots thy beauty, as frosts do bite the meads,

Confounds thy fame, as whirlwinds shake fair buds,

And in no sense is meet, or amiable.

A woman mov'd is like a fountain troubled,

Muddy, ill-seeming, thick, bereft of beauty;

And, while it is so, none so dry or thirsty

Will deign to sip, or touch one drop of it.

Thy husband is thy lord, thy life, thy keeper,

Thy head, thy sovereign; one that cares for thee,

And for thy maintenance; commits his body

To painful labour, both by sea and land,

To watch the night in storms, the day in cold,

Whilst thou liest warm at home, secure and safe;

And craves no other tribute at thy hands,

But love, fair looks, and true obedience,

Too little payment for so great a debt,

Such duty as the subject owes the prince,

Even such a woman oweth to her husband;

And when she's froward, peevish, sullen, sour,

And not obedient to his honest will,

What is she but a foul contending rebel,

And graceless traitor to her loving lord? –

I am asham'd that women are so simple

To offer war, where they should kneel for peace;

Or seek for rule, supremacy, and sway,

When they are bound to serve, love, and obey.

Why are our bodies soft, and weak, and smooth,

Unapt to toil and trouble in the world,

But that our soft conditions, and our hearts,

Should well agree with our external parts?

Come, come, you froward and unable worms,

My mind hath been as big as one of yours,

My heart as great, my reason, haply, more

To bandy word for word, and frown for frown;

But now I see, our lances are but straws,

Our strength as weak, our weakness past compare, -

That seeming to be most, which we indeed least are.

Then vail your stomachs, for it is no boot,

And place your hands below your husband's foot:

In token of which duty, if he please,

My hand is ready; may it do him ease.

THE MERCHANT OF VENICE

The Merchant of Venice is a romantic comedy. However, there are some very serious themes within the play regarding money, attempted murder, mercy and antisemitism. The play takes place in Venice, Italy. A merchant, named Antonio, wishes to lend his best friend, Bassanio, enough money (three thousand ducats) to woo the heiress, Portia. He borrows this money from the Jewish moneylender, Shylock. Shylock hates all Christians due to the ill treatment of Jews over the centuries. To make matters worse, his own daughter, Jessica, has fallen in love with a Christian, and later runs away with him. He agrees to lend the money to Antonio on condition that he signs an agreement that if the money is not paid after three months, Shylock can lawfully cut off a pound of Antonio's flesh.

Meanwhile, in Belmont, the beautiful heiress, Portia is receiving foreign suitors. The only suitor she is interested in is, the Venetian, Bassanio. A task has been set for these suitors to choose one of three caskets of gold, silver and lead. Portia's future husband will be the suitor who chooses the right casket which has her portrait inside it. Portia tries to delay Bassanio's choosing of the casket, concerned that he might fail to choose the right casket. Bassanio eventually chooses the lead casket, which includes the portrait of Portia.

Later in the play, Shylock learns that Antonio's ships have been wrecked and he is no longer able to repay the loan. This results in a lengthy Trial Scene where Shylock is determined to claim his revenge. However, Portia, desperate to save the situation, disguises herself as an out of town lawyer and saves the day on a technicality. She requests that Shylock act mercifully but Shylock refuses. He is determined to pursue his case according to Venetian law. Portia reminds Shylock that he will, in fact, be breaking Venetian law if he takes more than just a pound of flesh. He must not shed any blood in the transaction. If he does, by law, all his goods will be confiscated. Shylock has lost his case. All is resolved. Portia and Bassanio are wed. Her lady in waiting, Nerissa marries Gratiano and Jessica marries Lorenzo.

THE MERCHANT OF VENICE ACT 1, SC 2

(Portia is discussing her need to find a suitable suitor with her waiting woman, Nerissa).

Portia:

By my troth, Nerissa, my little body is aweary of this great world.

Good sentences and well pronounced.

If to do were as easy as to know what were good to do, chapels had been churches, poor men's cottages princes' palaces. I can easier teach what were good to do than be one of the twenty to follow mine own teaching. But this reasoning is not in the fashion to choose me a husband. O me, the word 'choose'! I may neither choose who I would, nor refuse who I dislike. Is it not hard, Nerissa, that I cannot choose one nor refuse none?

I pray thee, over-name these suitors and as thou namest them I will describe them; and according to my description level at my affection.

The Neapolitan Prince?

Ay, that's a colt indeed, for he doth nothing but talk of his horse; and that he can shoe him himself!

The French lord, Monsieur Le Bon?

God made him, and therefore let him pass as a man. In truth, I know it is a sin to be a mocker, but he! If I should marry him I should marry twenty husbands. If he would despise me, I would forgive him; for if he love me to madness, I shall never requite him.

Falconbridge, the young baron of England?

You know I say nothing to him, for he hath neither Latin, French nor Italian; and you will come into the court and swear that I have a poor pennyworth in English. He is a proper man's picture; but alas who can converse with a dumb-show?

The young German, the Duke of Saxony's nephew?

Very vilely in the morning when he is sober, and most vilely in the afternoon when he is drunk; when he is best, he is little worse than a man and when he is worst, he is little better than a beast. I hope I shall make shift to go without him!

Therefore, for fear the worst, I pray thee set a deep glass of Rhenish wine on the contrary casket, for if the devil be within, and temptation without, I know he will choose it.

If I live to be as old as Sibylla, I will die as chaste as Diana unless I be obtained by the manner of my father's will. I am glad this parcel of wooers are so reasonable; for there is not one among them but I dote on his very absence; and I pray God grant them a fair departure.

THE MERCHANT OF VENICE ACT 3 SC 2

(Portia is talking to Bassanio regarding choosing the caskets which her father has set her to determine whom she should marry).

Portia:

I pray you, tarry; pause a day or two,

Before you hazard; for, in choosing wrong

I lose your company; therefore, forbear a while:

There's something tells me, (but it is not love,)

I would not lose you; and you know yourself,

Hate counsels not in such a quality:

But lest you should not understand me well,

(And yet a maiden hath no tongue but thought,)

I would detain you here some month or two,

Before you venture for me. I could teach you

How to choose right, but then I am forsworn;

So will I never be: so may you miss me;

But if you do, you'll make me wish a sin,

That I had been forsworn. Beshrew your eyes,

They have o'er-looked me, and divided me;

One half of me is yours, the other half yours, -

Mine own, I would say; but if mine, then yours,

And so all yours: O! these naughty times

Put bars between the owners and their rights;

And so, though yours, not yours. – Prove it so,

Let fortune go to hell for it, - not I.

I speak too long; but 't is to peize the time;

To eke it, and to draw it out in length,

To stay you from election.

THE MERCHANT OF VENICE ACT 3 SC 2

(Bassanio has just chosen the 'right' casket which will enable him to marry Portia. Portia responds to Bassanio as her future husband).

Portia:

You see me, Lord Bassanio, where I stand,

Such as I am. Though for myself alone

I would not be ambitious in my wish

To wish myself much better, yet for you

I would be trebled twenty times myself,

A thousand times more fair, ten thousand times

More rich, that only to stand high in your account

I might in virtues, beauties, livings, friends,

Exceed account. But the full sum of me

Is sum of something which, to term in gross,

Is an unlessoned girl, unschooled, unpractised,

Happy in this, she is not yet so old

But she may learn; happier than this,

She is not bred so dull but she can learn;

Happiest of all is that her gentle spirit

Commits itself to yours to be directed

As from her lord, her governor, her king.

Myself and what is mine to you and yours

Is now converted. But now I was the lord

Of this fair mansion, master of my servants,

Queen o'er myself; and even now, but now,

This house, these servants, and this same myself

Are yours, my lord's. I give them with this ring,

Which when you part from, lose, or give away,

Let it presage the ruin of your love.

MERCHANT OF VENICE ACT 4, SCENE I

(The Court Scene. Portia, disguised as a lawyer (named Belario) confronts, the Jew, Shylock. She asks him to be merciful).

Portia:

Which is the merchant here? And which the Jew?

(To Shylock) Is your name Shylock?

Of a strange nature is the suit you follow,

Yet in such rule, that the Venetian law

Cannot impugn you as you do proceed.

(To Antonio) You stand within his danger do you not?

Do you confess the bond?

Then must the Jew be merciful.

I pray you, let me look upon the bond.

Shylock there's thrice thy money off'red thee.

Why this bond is forfeit,

And lawfully by this the Jew may claim a pound of flesh

A pound of flesh, to be by him cut off

Nearest the merchant's heart: be merciful,

Take thrice thy money, bid me tear the bond.

(To Antonio)   Why then thus it is -

You must prepare your bosom for his knife.

Therefore, lay bare your bosom.

Are there balance here to weigh

The flesh? *(Portia now addresses Shylock)*

Have by some surgeon Shylock on your charge,

To stop his wounds, lest he do bleed to death.

(To Antonio)

You merchant, have you anything to say?

(To Shylock)

A pound of that same merchant's flesh is thine,

The court awards it, and the law doth give it.

And you must cut this flesh from off his breast,

The law allows it, and the court awards it.

Tarry a little, there is something else,-

This bond doth give thee here no jot of blood,

The words expressly are 'a pound of flesh':

Take then thy bond, take thou thy pound of flesh,

But in the cutting it, if thou dost shed

One drop of Christian blood, thy lands and goods

Are (by the laws of Venice) confiscate

Unto the state of Venice.

Thyself shalt see the act:

For as thou urgest justice, be assur'd

Thou shalt have justice more than thou desir'st.

The Jew shall have all justice - soft no haste!

He shall have nothing but the penalty.

Therefore, prepare thee to cut off the flesh-

Shed thou no blood, nor cut thou less nor more

But just a pound of flesh: if thou tak'st more

Or less than just a pound, be it but so much

As makes it light or heavy in the substance,

Or the division of the twentieth part

Of one poor scruple, nay if the scale do turn

But in the estimation of a hair,

Thou diest, and all thy goods are confiscate.

Why doth the Jew pause? Take thy forfeiture.

He hath refused it in open court,

He shall have merely justice and his bond.

Thou shalt have nothing but the forfeiture

To be so taken at thy peril Jew.

AS YOU LIKE IT

As You Like It is a romantic comedy most of which is set in the Forest of Arden. There are two Dukes. The older, more popular Duke, has been banished by the younger, Duke Frederick. He has a daughter called Rosalind. Duke Frederick's daughter is called Celia. The two girls are inseparable. The Duke decides to banish Rosalind due to her popularity and on hearing this, Celia decides to accompany her. Rosalind disguises herself as a boy, for safety and they take the fool, Touchstone with them. Prior to this banishment, Rosalind has fallen in love with Orlando who has also had to run away to the forest to escape his jealous, older brother, Oliver. Whilst in the forest, Rosalind discovers that Orlando is there too but cannot pursue a relationship with him as she is now in disguise. Much comedy ensues due to mistaken identity. Later, when Rosalind discovers that Orlando has been injured trying to save his brother, Oliver, from a lion, Rosalind faints and reveals herself. Oliver redeems himself and falls in love with Celia. Touchstone marries Audrey and the shepherds, Phoebe and Silvius also marry. Duke Frederick, on seeking out his brother in order to murder him, is converted by a hermit and decides to leave his Dukedom to the old Duke. A large wedding takes place and everyone lives happily ever after.

AS YOU LIKE IT ACT 1, SC 2

(Celia is upset by the fact, that her best friend and cousin, Rosalind, has been banished from the Court, by her father, Duke Frederick.)

Celia:

O my poor Rosalind, whither wilt thou go?

Wilt thou change fathers? I will give thee mine.

I charge thee, be not thou more grieved than I am.

Prithee, be cheerful; knowest thou not the Duke

Hath banished me, his daughter?

No, hath not? Rosalind lacks then the love

Which teacheth thee that thou and I am one.

Shall we be sundered? Shall we part, sweet girl?

No, let my father seek another heir.

Therefore, devise with me how we may fly,

Whither to go, and what to bear with us,

And do not seek to take your change upon you,

To bear your griefs yourself and leave me out;

For, by this heaven, now at our sorrows pale,

Say what thou canst, I'll go along with thee.

To seek my uncle in the Forest of Arden.

I'll put myself in poor and mean attire

And with a kind of umber smirch my face.

The like do you; so shall we pass along

And never stir assailants.

What shall I call thee when thou art a man?

And therefore look, I'll call you 'Ganymede'.

No longer 'Celia', but 'Aliena'.

       Let's away

And get out jewels and our wealth together,

Devise the fittest time and safest way

To hide us from pursuit that will be made

After my flight. Now go in we content

To liberty, and not to banishment.

AS YOU LIKE IT ACT 3 SC 2

(Rosalind overhears the shepherdess, Phoebe, insulting the shepherd, Silvius, and decides to put Phoebe in her place. Phoebe immediately develops a crush on Rosalind, believing her to be a man).

Rosalind:

And why, I pray you?

Who might be your mother,

That you insult, exult, and all at once,

Over the wretched?

What though you have no beauty –

As, by my faith, I see no more in you

Than without candle may go dark to bed –

Must you be therefore proud and pitiless?

Why, what means this? Why do you look on me?

I see no more in you than in the ordinary

Of nature's sale-work. 'Ods my little life,

I think she means to tangle my eyes too!

No, faith, proud mistress, hope not after it:

'Tis not your inky brows, your black silk hair,

Your bugle eyeballs, nor your cheek of cream,

That can entame my spirits to your worship.

You foolish shepherd, wherefore do you follow her,

Like foggy south puffing with wind and rain?

You are a thousand times a properer man

Than she a woman: 'tis such fools as you

That makes the world full of ill-favored children:

'Tis not her glass, but you, that flatters her;

And out of you she sees herself more proper

Than any of her lineaments can show her.

But mistress, know yourself: down on your knees

And thank heaven, fasting, for a good man's love:

For I must tell you friendly in your ear,

Sell when you can: you are not for all markets:

Cry the man mercy; love him; take his offer:

Foul is most foul, being foul to be a scoffer.

So, take her to thee, shepherd: fare you well.

He's fallen in love with her foulness, and she'll fall in love with my anger. If it be so, as fast as she answers thee with frowning looks, I'll sauce her with bitter words. – Why look you so upon me?

I pray you, do not fall in love with me,

For I am falser than vows made in wine;

Besides, I like you not. If you will know my house,

'T is at the tuft of olives, here hard by. –

        Shepherd, ply her hard. –

        Shepherdess, look on him better,

        And be not proud; though all the world could see,

        None could be so abused in sight as he.

AS YOU LIKE IT ACT 3, SC 5

(Phoebe, a shepherdess, is speaking to Silvius, a shepherd in love with her. However, Phoebe has just met Rosalind disguised as Ganymede and is infatuated with him)!

Phoebe:

Pity you? Why, I am sorry for thee, gentle Silvius.

Thou hast my love; is not that neighbourly?

Silvius, the time was that I hated thee;

And yet it is not that I bear thee love:

But since that thou canst talk of love so well,

Thy company, which erst was irksome to me,

I will endure; and I'll employ thee too:

But do not look for further recompense

Than thine own gladness that thou art employed.

(Referring to Rosalind/Ganymede).

Know'st thou the youth that spoke to me ere while?

Think not I love him, though I ask for him;

'Tis but a peevish boy: yet he talks well;-

But what care I for words? yet words do well,

When he that speaks them pleases those that hear.

it is a pretty youth: - not very pretty: -

But, sure, he's proud; and yet his pride becomes him:

He'll make a proper man! The best thing in him

Is his complexion; and faster than his tongue

Did make offence, his eye did heal it up.

He is not very tall; yet for his years he's tall:

His leg is but so so; and yet 'tis well:

There was a pretty redness in his lip;

A little riper and more lusty red

Than that mixed in his cheek; 't was just the difference

Betwixt the constant red and mingled damask.

There be some women, Silvius, had they marked him

In parcels as I did, would have gone near

To fall in love with him: but, for my part,

I love him not, nor hate him not; and yet

I have more cause to hate him than to love him;

For what had he to do to chide at me?

He said, mine eyes were black, and mine hair black;

And now, I am remembered, scorned at me:

I marvel why I answered not again:

But that's all one; omittance is no quittance.

I'll write to him a very taunting letter,

And thou shalt bear it: wilt thou, Silvius?

I'll write it straight;

The matter's in my head, and in my heart:

I will be bitter with him, and passing short.

Go with me, Silvius.

AS YOU LIKE IT ACT 3, SC. 2

(Rosalind, dressed as a boy named Ganymede, is teasing Orlando. Orlando has been writing poetry for Rosalind and hanging the verses on the trees in the forest).

Rosalind:

There is a man who haunts the forest, that abuses our young plants with carving "Rosalind" on their barks; hangs odes upon hawthorns, and elegies on brambles; all, forsooth, deifying the name of Rosalind: if I could meet that fancy-monger, I would give him some counsel, for he seems to have the quotidian of love upon him.

My uncle taught me how to know a man in love: a lean cheek which you have not; an unquestionable spirit, which you have not; a beard neglected, which you have not: but I pardon you for that, for simply, your beard is a younger brother's revenue. Then, your hose should be ungartered, your bonnet unbanded, your sleeve unbuttoned, your shoe untied, and everything about you demonstrating a careless desolation.

But, in good sooth, are you he that hangs the verses on the trees, wherein Rosalind is so admired?

Love is merely a madness, and, I tell you, deserves as well a dark house and a whip as madmen do; and the reason why they are not so punished and cured is, that the lunacy is so ordinary that the whippers are in love too.

Yet I profess curing it by counsel.

I cured one so, and in this manner. He was to imagine me his love, his mistress; and I set him every day to woo me. At which time would I being but a moonish youth, grieve, be effeminate, changeable, longing and liking; proud, fantastical, apish, shallow, inconstant, full of tears, full of smiles, for every passion something, and for no passion truly anything, as boys and women are, for the most part, cattle of this colour; would now like him, now loathe him; then entertain him, then forswear him; now weep for him, then spit at him; that I drove my suitor from his mad humour of love to a living humour of madness, which was, to forswear the full stream of the world, and to live in a nook merely monastic.

And thus, I cured him, and this way will I take upon me to wash your liver as clean as a sound sheep's heart, that there shall not be one spot of love in't.

I would cure you, if you would but call me 'Rosalind', and come every day to my cote, and woo me.

A MIDSUMMER NIGHT'S DREAM

A Midsummer Night's Dream is a magical play, most of which takes place in forest outside Athens. The play opens in Theseus's court, in Athens. Egeus, Hermia's father is demanding that Hermia marries a young man named Demetrius. However, Hermia is in love with Lysander. This is where the trouble begins! Helena, meanwhile, loves Demetrius and when she learns that Hermia and Lysander are planning to run away together, Helena uses this opportunity to inform Demetrius, hoping that his affections will turn towards her.

From this point onwards, the play is set in the forest. It is midsummer's night, the only time when spirits and mortals are able to see each other. The spirit world spies on the human world and when Oberon spots Demetrius treating Helena badly, he decides to resolve this by sending his spirit Puck, to squeeze a magical love juice into Demetrius's eyes to force him to fall in love with her. However, the mischievous Puck, mistakenly squeezes the love juice into Lysander's eyes and so Lysander consequently falls in love with Helena. This all takes place in the middle of the play and results in a hilarious quarrel between the four lovers. Helena now has two men in love with her and poor Hermia is left very confused.

There is also a sub-plot which involves a group of Athenian workers who are rehearsing a play for the Duke of Athen's wedding. Their play rehearsals are extremely amusing and Bottom falls prey to the love juice too and, much to everyone's amusement, ends up being seduced by the Queen of the fairies, Titania.

As in all comedies, there is a happy ending. The play is selected to be performed at the wedding party of Theseus and Hippolyta. The four lovers are reunited with each other ie. Hermia and Lysander are married alongside Helena and Demetrius and all troubles in the forest are quickly forgotten. After all, it was merely a dream!

A MIDSUMMER NIGHT'S DREAM ACT 2, SC 1

(Titania berates Oberon's jealousy over the Indian boy).

Titania:

These are the forgeries of jealousy:

And never, since the middle summer's spring,

Met we on hill, in dale, forest, or mead,

By paved fountain, or by rushy brook,

Or in the beached margent of the sea,

To dance our ringlets to the whistling wind,

But with thy brawls thou hast disturb'd our sport.

Therefore the winds, piping to us in vain,

As in revenge, have suck'd up from the sea

Contagious fogs which, falling in the land,

Hath every pelting river made so proud

That they have overborne their continents:

The ox hath therefore stretch'd his yoke in vain,

The ploughman lost his sweat, and the green corn

Hath rotted ere his youth attain'd a beard:

The fold stands empty in the drowned field,

And crows are fatted with the murrion flock;

The nine-men's-morris is fill'd up with mud,

And the quaint mazes in the wanton green

For lack of tread are undistinguishable.

The human mortals want their winter cheer:

No night is now with hymn or carol blest.

Therefore the moon, the governess of floods,

Pale in her anger, washes all the air,

That rheumatic diseases do abound:

And thorough this distemperature we see

The seasons alter: hoary-headed frosts

Fall in the fresh lap of the crimson rose,

And on old Hiems' thin and icy crown

An odorous chaplet of sweet summer buds

Is, as in mockery, set. The spring, the summer,

The childing autumn, angry winter, change

Their wonted liveries, and the mazed world,

By their increase, now knows not which is which

And this same progeny of evils comes

From our debate, from our dissension:

We are their parents and original.

A MIDSUMMER NIGHT'S DREAM ACT 3, SC 1

(Titania, Queen of the Fairies, has been put under a spell to make her fall in love with the first thing she lays eyes on upon awakening. This happens to be the Mechanical, Bottom, who has also had a spell put upon him and is sporting a pair of asses ears).

Titania:

What angel wakes me from my flowery bed?

I pray thee, gentle mortal, sing again!

Mine ear is much enamour'd of thy note;

So is mine eye enthralled to thy shape;

And thy fair virtue's force, perforce, doth move me,

On the first view, to say, to swear, I love thee.

Thou art as wise as thy art beautiful.

Out of this wood do not desire to go:

Thou shalt remain here, whether thou wilt or no.

I am a spirit of no common rate;

The summer still doth tend upon my state;

And I do love thee: therefore, go with me:

I'll give you fairies to attend on thee,

And they shall fetch thee jewels from the deep,

And sing, while thou on pressed flowers dost sleep:

And I will purge thy mortal grossness so

That thou shalt like an airy spirit go.

(She speaks to four fairies)

Pease-blossom! Cobweb! Moth! And Mustard-seed!

Be kind and courteous to this gentle-man;

Hop in his walks, and gambol in his eyes;

Feed him with apricocks and dewberries,

With purple grapes, green figs, and mulberries.

The honey-bags steal from the honey-bees,

And for night-tapers crop their waxen thighs,

And light them at the fiery glow-worm's eyes:

Nod to him, elves, do him courtesies.

Come, wait upon him; lead him to my bower.

The moon methinks, looks with a watery eye;

And when she weeps, weeps every little flower,

Lamenting some enforced chastity.

Tie up my love's tongue, bring him silently.

A MIDSUMMER NIGHT'S DREAM ACT 3, SC 2

(Helena believes that Hermia, Lysander and Demetrius are plotting against her).

Helena:

Lo, she is one of this confederacy!

Now I perceive they have conjoin'd all three

To fashion this false sport, in spite of me.

Injurious Hermia, most ungrateful maid!

Have you conspired, have you with these contrived

To bait me with this foul derision?

Is all the counsel that we two have shared,

The sisters' vows, the hours that we have spent,

When we have chid the hasty-footed time

For parting us, - O, is all forgot?

All school days' friendship, all childhood innocence?

We, Hermia, like two artificial gods,

Have with our needles created both one flower,

Both on one sampler, sitting on one cushion,

Both warbling of one song, both in one key,

As if our hands, our sides, voices and minds,

Had been incorporate. So we grew together,

Like to a double cherry, seeming parted,

But yet an union in partition;

Two lovely berries moulded on one stem;

So, with two seeming bodies, but one heart;

Two of the first, like coats in heraldry,

Due but to one and crowned with one crest.

And will you rent our ancient love asunder,

To join with men in scorning your poor friend?

It is not friendly, 'tis not maidenly:

Our sex, as well as I, may chide you for it,

Though I alone do feel the injury.

Have you not set Lysander, as in scorn,

To follow me and praise my eyes and face?

And made your other love Demetrius,

Who even but now did spurn me with his foot,

To call me goddess, nymph, divine and rare,

Precious, celestial? Wherefore speaks he this

To her he hates? And wherefore doth Lysander

Deny your love, so rich within his soul,

And tender me, forsooth, affection,

But by your setting on, by your consent?

What though I be not so in grace as you,

So hung upon with love, so fortunate,

But miserable most, to love unloved?

This you should pity rather than despise.

Aye, do, persever, counterfeit sad looks,

Make mouths upon me when I turn my back;

Wink each at other; hold the sweet jest up:

This sport, well carried, shall be chronicled.

If you have any pity, grace, or manners,

You would not make me such an argument.

But fare ye well; 't is partly my own fault,

Which death or absence soon shall remedy.

THE WINTER'S TALE

The play takes place in Sicily where the King Leontes is entertaining his childhood friend, the King of Bohemia, Polixenes. When it is time for him to leave, both Leontes and his wife Hermione, try to persuade him to stay longer. The friends are close but Leontes becomes unreasonably jealous of his wife's ease with his former friend, Polixenes and obsesses that they are in love with one another. He even tells their small son that his mother has always been unfaithful. He orders one of his lords, Camillo, to murder Polixenes. Camillo, believing there to be no truth in this accusation, warns Polixenes and runs away with him. Believing this to be a sign of their guilt, Leontes imprisons his wife. Paulina, a gentle-women takes care of her whilst in prison. Hermione gives birth to a baby girl and convinced that the child is not his, Leontes orders Paulina's husband, Antigonus, to get rid of the child and leave it where it can die. Leontes holds a public trial for his wife where Hermione defends herself with grace and sincerity but Leontes still refuses to believe her. During the trial, news arrives that their little son is dead from the grief of missing his mother. Hermione faints and her ladies take her away. Leontes starts to feel remorse and tells them to treat her kindly but Paulina, being angry with him, returns to tell him that Hermione is now dead.

The abandoned baby girl is found by a shepherd far away in Bohemia and is brought up as his own child and named Perdita. He also looks after a young boy named Florizel, who is actually the King of Bohemia's son and therefore a prince. Sixteen years have passed and Perdita has grown very fond of Florizel, who she considers a step-brother. The King, Polixenes, Florizel's father, arrives disguised as a pedlar. He has come to check the wellbeing of his son. When Florizel announces his intentions to marry the beautiful Perdita, the 'pedlar' removes his disguise revealing himself as the King. He declares that his son will not marry a simple peasant girl and storms off. The shepherd is afraid of upsetting his King and confesses that Perdita is not his true daughter but that she was found abandoned as a young baby. Florizel and Perdita decide to run away together. They set sail for Sicily. Back in Sicily, for sixteen years, Leontes has been grieving the loss of his family. He receives the runaways, Florizel and Perdita at his Palace and is strangely attracted and fond of them. Meanwhile, Polixenes, in pursuit of his son, also travels to Sicily. The shepherd reveals the truth of Perdita's identity and has a Royal letter to prove it. Leontes is full of joy at the discovery of his long-lost daughter but equally distraught regarding the fate of his late wife, Hermione. Pauline then suggests that Leontes goes to her house where she has a statue of the late Hermione. In reality, it is actually Hermione who has been in hiding and is very much alive and delighted to be reunited with her daughter. Paulina is offered a hand in marriage to Camillo and the two kings are united by the marriage of Perdita and Florizel.

THE WINTER'S TALE ACT 3 SC 2

(Hermione pleads her innocence in front of the court).

Hermione:

Since what I am about to say must be that

Which contradicts my accusation and

The testimony on my part no other

But what comes from myself, it shall scarce boot me

To say Not Guilty: mine integrity

Being counted falsehood, shall as I express it,

Be so received. But this: if powers divine

Behold our human actions, as they do,

I doubt not then but innocence shall make

False accusation blush and tyranny

Tremble at patience. You, my lord, best know,

Who least will seem to do so, my past life

Hath been as continent, as chaste, as true,

As I am now unhappy: which is more

Than history can pattern, though devised

And played to take spectators. For behold me

A fellow of the royal bed, which owe

A moiety of the throne, a great king's daughter,

The mother to a hopeful prince, here standing

To prat and talk for life and honor fore

Who please to come and hear. For life I prize it

As I weigh grief, which I would spare: for honor,

Tis a derivative from me to mine,

And only that can I stand for. I appeal

To your own conscience sir, before Polixenes

Came to court, how I was in your grace,

How merited to be so: since he came

With what encounter so uncurrent,

Have strained to appear thus: if one jot beyond

The bound of honor, or in act or will

That way inclining, hardened be the hearts

Of all that hear me, and my near'st of kin

Cry fie upon my grave.

MEASURE FOR MEASURE

Measure for Measure is a comedy with some very serious themes within it. The play takes place in Vienna where the Duke, Vincentio, is planning to leave the city, leaving his deputy, Angelo and an older lord, Escalus, in charge. Actually, the Duke does not leave Vienna but remains in the city in disguise hoping to see if his Deputy can improve things there. There is much unrest in Vienna and laws are being flouted. Angelo plans to re-establish the law of the land and tighten things up harshly. There is a young gentleman named Claudio who is in love with a young girl named Juliet. Their marriage plans have been delayed and Juliet is already pregnant. Claudio believes that his marriage contract to Juliet should suffice but Angelo passes the death sentence on Claudio as he has broken the law. He is to be put to death in three days. Claudio appeals against this judgement as he feels that he has done no less wrong than many others in the city and turns to his sister, Isabella, for help. Isabella is an honest woman, training to be a nun and Claudio thinks her honest reputation may convince Angelo to change his mind. Isabella, whilst morally judgemental of her brother, also loves him dearly and is prepared to beg Angelo for his release. Angelo is rigid in his rule and issues punishments severely despite Escalus suggesting he act with more tolerance.

When Isabella visits Angelo to plead for her brother's freedom, Angelo falls in love with her and tries to strike a bargain that if Isabella will sleep with him, he will release her brother. Isabella is horrified at the thought and at Angelo's double standards. She wants to free her brother but cannot compromise her virginity. Initially, her brother understands that she cannot do this but in desperation begs her to reconsider. The Duke, in disguise as a friar at the prison, overhears their conversation and concocts a plan. A woman named Mariana is in love with Angelo and was engaged to him. Unfortunately, she lost her dowry and Angelo was not prepared to marry her. He will ask her to swap places with Isabella. Isabella is naturally relieved and agrees with the plan to change places that night. They arrange to meet in an enclosed garden. Mariana is more than happy to meet with Angelo as she already has a pre-marriage contract with Angelo. However, Angelo, with double standards, does not keep his promise regarding Claudio and sends orders for him to be beheaded immediately. Fortunately, another prisoner has died that day and it is his head which is sent as 'proof' to Angelo. Even Isabella believes her brother has been beheaded. The Duke then plans his return to Vienna. On arrival, Isabella presents the Duke with a petition accusing Angelo of mal practice. Mariana speaks against him too. However, the arrogant Angelo accuses the two women of lying and the Duke pretends to believe him. Then the Duke returns disguised as a Friar in defence of the two women. The Duke then reveals his true identity and sentences Angelo to death as being justice for killing Claudio. Both women plead for Angelo to be spared. The Duke agrees as Claudio is in fact very much alive and Mariana is happy now that she can be married to Angelo. The Duke then asks Isabella for her hand in marriage.

MEASURE FOR MEASURE ACT 2 SC 4

(Isabella pleads for her brother's life. His only crime is loving Juliet. She is talking to Angelo, begging him to spare her brother).

<u>Isabella:</u>

My brother did love Juliet

And you tell me that he shall die for't.

I know your virtue hath a licence in't

Which seems a little fouler than it is

To pluck on others.

Ha! Little honour to be much believed,

And most pernicious purpose. Seeming, seeming.

I will proclaim thee, Angelo, look for't.

Sign me a present pardon for my brother,

Or with an outstretched throat I'll tell the world aloud

What man thou art.

<u>Angelo:</u>   Who will believe thee, Isabel?

(Angelo then asks Isabella to sleep with him in return for her brother's freedom & give him her answer by tomorrow. Angelo exits).

<u>Isabella</u>: *(alone on stage).*

To whom should I complain? Did I tell this

Who would believe me? Oh, perilous mouths

That bear in them one and the self-same tongue,

Either of condemnation or aproof,

Bidding the law make curtsey to their will,

Hooking both right and wrong to th'appetite

To follow as it draws. I'll to my brother.

Though he hath fall'n by prompture of the blood

Yet hath he in him such a mind of honour

That had he twenty heads, to tender down

On twenty bloody blocks he'd yield them up

Before his sister should her body stoop

To such abhorred pollution.

Then Isabel live chaste, and brother die:

More than our brother is our chastity.

I'll tell him yet of Angelo's request,

And fit his mind to death for his soul's rest.

HENRY VI PART 1

Henry VI is a trilogy and covers the War of the Roses. The young son of Henry V succeeds to the throne and becomes Henry VI, protected by Duke Humphrey. The English are still involved in battles in France. The French eventually win the battle against the English largely through the help of Joan of Arc, whom the English to believe to be a sorceress. Joan of Arc is later burned at the stake. At home, there is a quarrel between the Lord Protector (Duke Humphrey) and the Cardinal of Winchester. There is civil unrest. Richard Plantagenet is made Duke of York. Richard Plantagenet is making claims to the crown and his followers wear white roses to represent the House of York and the House of Lancaster wear red roses. There are ongoing battles in different regions of France, but Henry craves peace. The earl of Suffolk has fallen in love with a beautiful, penniless Frenchwoman named Margaret of Anjou but as he is already married, offers her to the King instead. Henry marries Margaret but he is weak and Margaret is strong willed and is still in love with the Earl of Suffolk.

HENRY 6TH PART 1 ACT 3 SC 3

(Joan has persuaded the Duke of Burgundy to remain loyal to the French cause. Formerly the Duke has sided with the English).

JOAN:

Brave Burgundy, undoubted hope of France,

Stay. Let thy humble handmaid speak to thee.

Look on thy country, look on fertile France,

And see the cities and the towns defaced

By wasting ruin of the cruel foe.

As looks the mother on her lowly babe

When death doth close his tender-dying eyes,

See, see the pining malady of France;

Behold the wounds, the most unnatural wounds,

Which thou thyself hast given her woeful breasts.

O turn thy edged sword another way,

Strike those that hurt, and hurt not those that help.

One drop of blood drawn from thy country's bosom

Should grieve thee more than streams of foreign gore.

Return thee, therefore, with a flood of tears,

And wash away thy country's stained spots.

Besides, all French and France exclaims on thee,

Doubting thy birth and lawful progeny.

Who join'st thou with, but with a lordly nation

That will not trust thee but for profit's sake?

When Talbot hath set footing once in France

And fashioned thee that instrument of ill,

Who then but English Henry will be lord,

And thou be thrust out like a fugitive?

Call we to mind, and mark but this for proof:

Was not the Duke of Orleans thy foe?

And was he not in England prisoner?

But when they heard he was thine enemy

They set him free, without his ransom paid,

In spite of Burgundy and all his friends.

See, then, thou fight'st against thy countrymen,

And join'st with them will be thy slaughtermen.

Come, come, return; return, thou wandering lord,

Charles and the rest will take thee in their arms.

HENRY 6th PART 1, ACT 1 Sc 2

(Joan of Arc tells the Dauphin of her vision to help the French army claim victory against the English).

La Pucelle (Joan):

(The courtiers are trying to trick Joan into believing that another person is the Dauphin, but Joan cannot be fooled).

Where is the Dauphin? - Come, come from behind;

I know thee well, though never seen before.

Be not amaz'd, there is nothing hid from me:

In private will I talk with thee apart,

Stand back, you lords, and give us leave a while.

(She speaks to the Dauphin)

Dauphin, I am by birth a shepherd's daughter,

My wit untrain'd in any kind of art.

Heaven and our Lady gracious hath it pleas'd

To shine on my contemptible estate:

Lo! Whilst I waited on my tender lambs,

And to sun's parching head display'd my cheeks,

God's mother deigned to appear to me;

And, in a vision full of majesty,

Will'd me to leave my based vocation,

And free my country from calamity.

Her aid she promis'd and assur'd success:

In complete glory she reveal'd herself;

And, whereas I was black and swart before,

With those clear rays, which she infus'd on me,

That beauty am I bless'd with, which you see.

Ask me what question thou canst possible,

And I will answer unpremeditated:

My courage try by combat, if thou dar'st,

And thou shalt find that I exceed my sex.

Resolve on this, - thou shalt be fortunate,

If thou receive me for thy warlike mate.

(Joan takes out her sword)

I am prepared. Here is my keen-edg'd sword,

Deck'd with five flower-de-luces on each side;

The which at Touraine, in Saint Katharine's churchyard,

Out of a great deal of old iron I chose forth.

(Joan fights with Charles, to show her strength).

Christ's mother helps me, else I were too weak.

I must not yield to any rites of love,

For my profession's sacred from above:

When I have chased all thy foes from hence,

Then will I think upon a recompense.

Assigned am I to be the English scourge.

This night the siege assuredly I'll raise:

Expect Saint Martin's summer, halcyon days,

Since I have entered into those wars.

Glory is like a circle in the water,

Which never ceaseth to enlarge itself,

Till, by broad spreading, it disperse to nought.

Wit Henry's death the English circle ends;

Dispersed are the glories it included.

Now am I like that proud insulting ship,

Which Caesar and his fortune bare at once.

MACBETH

Macbeth is a tragedy with a theme of ambition. Macbeth and his wife end up destroying themselves by craving the throne of Scotland by any means possible. Macbeth and friend, Banquo, two great captains, are returning from battle and meet three witches on a heath who prophesy greatness. Duncan is the current king and bestows a new title on Macbeth for his loyalty and bravery. Macbeth is now Thane of Glamis and Cawdor. The witches have prophesied that he will be King and this has set Macbeth's ambition racing. He cannot wait to tell his wife, Lady Macbeth. He sends a letter to her, in advance of his return, informing her of his news. The witches have also prophesied that Banquo will have kings. King Duncan informs Macbeth that he will be visiting Macbeth's castle and Macbeth is tempted to murder him despite having some reservations. Lady Macbeth persuades her husband to kill Duncan while he is sleeping and blame the drunken guards. Macbeth is fearful and starts to visualise a bloody dagger before him. Lady Macbeth urges him to carry out the deed and assists him by smearing the king's blood over the guards. Shortly afterwards, Lord Macduff arrives at the castle and on visiting Duncan in his bed chamber finds him dead. Macbeth kills the two guards before the truth can be discovered. The king's sons escape to England in fear of their lives but some believe their exit proves them guilty. Macbeth is crowned King. He arranges to have Banquo and his son murdered. Banquo may have suspicions about Macbeth. Banquo shouts a warning to his son to escape. At supper that evening, the ghost of Banquo appears. Only Macbeth can see him and his guests notice his alarming behaviour. Macbeth seeks out the witches once again and he is told to beware Macduff and he should fear no one born of woman. A third apparition assures him of success until the time Birnam wood comes to Dunsinane. He is then faced with a line of kings with Banquo smiling on. Macbeth learns that Macduff has left for England to raise an army and Macbeth sends his murderers to kill

Lady Macduff and her sons. Lady Macbeth is haunted by her evil deeds and begins to sleepwalk. She ends up killing herself. Macduff has raised an army of English and Scottish soldiers and march upon Dunsinane. They disguise themselves as a marching forest. Macbeth's disloyal soldiers abandon him and surrender to the oncoming army. Macduff seeks out Macbeth and they fight. Macbeth is slain as Macduff was 'not of woman born' but born by caesarean. Malcolm is crowned King and peace is restored to Scotland.

MACBETH ACT 4 SC 2

(Lady Macduff is speaking to Ross. Her young sons are with her. Macbeth has sent his soldiers to murder her).

LADY MACDUFF:

What had he done to make him fly the land?

His flight was madness. When our actions do not,

Our fears do make us traitors.

Wisdom! To leave his wife, to leave his babes,

His mansion, and his titles, in a place

From whence himself does fly? He loves us not;

He wants the natural touch; for the poor wren

The most diminutive of birds, will fight

Her young ones in her nest, against the owl.

All is the fear and nothing is the love;

As little is the wisdom, where the flight

So runs against all reason ... *(She draws her son to her side)*

Father'd he is, and yet he's fatherless.

(To her son)

Sirrah, your father's dead;

And what will you do now? How will you live?

Yes, he is dead. How wilt thou do for a father?

(She rises, as a messenger enters, and advises her to leave at once, with her children)

Whither should I fly?

I have done no harm. But I remember now

I am in this earthly world, where to do harm

Is often laudable, t'do good sometime

Accounted dangerous folly. Why then, alas.

Do I put up that womanly defence

To say I have done no harm?

(Enter murderers)

What are these faces?

Murderers!

MACBETH ACT 1, SC 5

(Inverness. Macbeth's Castle. Lady Macbeth is alone, reading a letter her husband has sent her regarding his meeting with the three witches).

<u>Lady Macbeth:</u>

(reading)
They met me in the day of success; and I have learned by the perfect'st report they have more in them than mortal knowledge. When I burned in desire to question them further, they made themselves air, into which they vanished. Whiles I stood rapt in the wonder of it, came missives from the King, who all-hailed me 'Thane of Cawdor'; by which title, before, these weird sisters saluted me, and referred me to the coming on of time, with 'Hail, King that shalt be!' This have I thought good to deliver thee, my dearest partner of greatness, that thou mightst not lose the dues of rejoicing, by being ignorant of what greatness is promised thee. Lay it to thy heart, and farewell.

Glamis, thou art, and Cawdor, and shalt be
What thou art promised. Yet do I fear thy nature;
It is too full o' th' milk of human kindness
To catch the nearest way. Thou wouldst be great,
Art not without ambition, but without
The illness should attend it. What thou wouldst highly,
That wouldst thou holily; wouldst not play false,
And yet wouldst wrongly win. Thou'dst have, great Glamis,
That which cries "Thus thou must do" if thou have it;
And that which rather thou dost fear to do
Than wishest should be undone. Hie thee hither,
That I may pour my spirits in thine ear,
And chastise with the valor of my tongue
All that impedes thee from the golden round
Which fate and metaphysical aid doth seem
To have thee crowned withal.

HENRY VI PART 3

This is the sequel to Henry VI Part II and continues the story of the battle of the War of the Roses. Richard, Duke of York has taken over Parliament house and has claimed the English throne for himself. Rather than battle, Henry VI wants to negotiate their differences through discussion. He accepts Richard as King as his own claim to the throne was tenuous. His wife, Queen Margaret, however, is furious and will not accept defeat. The Lancastrian Margaret and Richard, from the House of York, go into battle. The York's are outnumbered and Margaret, with her gallant Clifford, slaughter Richard, Duke of York along with other members of his family in revenge for the death of so many of their own relatives. Richard's sons, Edward and Richard continue the fight with the Earl of Warwick at the helm. Outside the city of York, Henry, a placid character, laments the death toll. It his wife Margaret who is the warmonger but as the battle progresses, she has to admit defeat. The House of York are victorious and Edward marches upon London. Henry is captured from hiding and is imprisoned. Edward bestows titles on his two brothers – Richard (later to become Richard III) becomes Duke of Gloucester and George, Duke of Clarence. Richard's ambition is evident very early on and he is determined that his physical deformity will not deter him. Edward falls in love with Elizabeth, Lady Grey. Warwick is furious at this marriage as he has already travelled to France to arrange for Edward to form an allegiance with the French princess. The Earl of Warwick changes sides and supports Queen Margaret who is already in France gaining support for the release of her husband, King Henry. Warwick offers his eldest daughter in marriage to Margaret's son. Together they will fight to regain the throne. The Duke of Clarence, then changes his allegiances as he is unhappy with his brother's marriage to Elizabeth Grey. The hunchback, Richard, remains loyal to his brother; he still has an eye on the throne for himself. As the armies prepare for battle,

Edward is captured whilst sleeping and Warwick places the crown on Henry's head. However, Henry has no interest in being king and hands over his duties to Warwick and the Duke of Clarence. He wants his wife and son returned from France. Richard, Duke of Gloucester, manages to free his brother, Edward, and sends him abroad for safe keeping where he musters up an army. Edward then returns to England to join Richard who re-capture Henry and lock him in the tower. On facing his brother Edward in battle, George, Duke of Clarence, finds he cannot fight against his own brother and swiftly changes allegiances. Warwick is killed but Margaret continues to fight until she is captured. Her son is brutally killed before her. Richard then goes to the tower to kill Henry. The House of Lancaster has been destroyed. Queen Elizabeth Grey, having taken sanctuary in Westminster Abbey, has given birth to a son who will later become Edward V of England. Queen Margaret is exiled to France.

KING HENRY 6TH, PART 3 ACT 1, SC 4

(Queen Margaret is on the battle field and seeks her revenge on York who has mercilessly killed many of Margaret's own family members).

Queen Margaret:

Brave warriors, Clifford and Northumberland,

Come, make him stand upon this molehill here,

That raught at mountains with outstretched arms,

Yet parted but the shadow with his hand. –

What, was it you that would be England's king?

Was't you that revell'd in our parliament,

And made a preachment of your high descent?

Where are your mess of sons to back you now?

The wanton Edward and the lusty George?

And where's that valiant crook-back prodigy,

Dicky your boy that with his grumbling voice

Was wont to cheer his dad in mutinies?

Or, with the rest, where is your darling Rutland?

Look, York: I stain'd this napkin with the blood

That valiant Clifford, with his rapier's point,

Made issue from the bosom of the boy;

And if thine eyes can water for his death,

I give thee this to dry thy cheeks withal.

Alas, poor York! But that I hate thee deadly,

I should lament thy miserable state.

I pr'thee, grieve to make me merry, York.

What hath thy fiery heart so parch'd thine entrails

That not a tear can fall for Rutland's death?

Why are thou patient, man? Thou shouldst be mad;

And I, to make thee mad, do mock thee thus.

Stamp, rave, and fret, that I may sing and dance.

Thou wouldst be fee'd, I see, to make me sport;

York cannot speak unless he wear a crown -

A crown for York! – and, lords, bow low to him -

Hold, you his hands whilst I do set it on.

(Putting a paper crown on his head)

Ay, marry, sir, now looks he like a king!

Ay, this is he that took King Henry's chair;

And this is he was his adopted heir. –

But how is it that great Plantagenet

Is crown'd so soon, and broke his solemn oath?

As I bethink me, you should not be king

Till our King Henry had shook hands with death.

And will you pale your head in Henry's glory,

And rob his temples of the diadem

Now in his life, against your holy oath?

O, 'tis a fault too, too unpardonable!-

Off with the crown; and, with the crown, his head;

And whilst we breathe take time to do him dead.

JULIUS CAESAR

The play is set in Rome during the reign of Julius Caesar. Caesar is a popular ruler but as in all political scenarios, his power is sometimes fragile, with those hungry for power plotting against him. There is a celebration in the streets and someone shouts out 'Beware the Ides of March'. There is a politician named Cassius, who is conspiring to assassinate Caesar. He tries to persuade the loyal and honourable Brutus and another man named, Casca, to join forces with him. Mark Antony is a great friend of Julius Caesar and he warns Caesar to be mindful of Cassius. Caesar dismisses Mark Antony's suggestions as he believes Cassius is incapable of plotting against him. Cassius plants some petitions citing citizen unrest and uses this information to convince Brutus to join him for the sake of the Roman Empire. Brutus is stricken with guilt over how he should proceed. Cassius wants to assassinate Mark Antony alongside Caesar. Brutus has his doubts and manages to dissuade his colleagues from doing so. The assassination is planned for 15th March (the Ides of March). Portia, Brutus's wife, is concerned at her husband's behaviour and eventually Brutus reveals the assassination plot to her. Caesar's wife is also fearful for her husband's and tries to persuade him not to go to the capitol that day. She has almost succeeded in persuading him when a conspirator ridicules his weakness of character. There are those who have overheard the conspiracy and attempt to intervene by slipping a note of warning to Caesar but unfortunately, he disregards it. Caesar is surrounded by the conspirators and is stabbed to death. Caesar notices his loyal friend, Brutus, amongst them. Mark Antony takes the helm, and slowly waits to avenge Caesar's murderers. A great orator, Mark Antony convinces the crowds that Brutus was responsible for Caesar's death. Gradually,the conspirators involved in Caesar's death are murdered. An army is gathered to fight against Brutus and Cassius once and for all. Missing her husband in the war and afraid of the consequences of the ensuing battles, Portia kills herself. Brutus and Cassius, whilst friends, have very different approaches in war. They disagree on strategy. One night, Brutus is visited by the ghost of Julius Caesar warning of his defeat. Cassius meanwhile, receives incorrect information regarding the battle and takes his own life. When Brutus realises he too is losing the battle he suffers the same fate as Cassius. Mark Antony wins the battle.

JULIUS CAESAR ACT 2 SC 1

(Brutus has been acting secretively. Portia begs her husband, Brutus, to confide in her).

Portia:

Is Brutus sick? And is it physical

To walk unbraced and suck up the humors

Of the dank morning? What, is Brutus sick?

And will he steal out of his wholesome bed

To dare the vile contagion of the night,

And tempt the rheumy and unpurged air

To add unto his sickness? No, my Brutus,

You have some sick offence within your mind,

Which by the right and virtue of my place

I ought to know of. And, upon my knees,

I charm you, by my once-commended beauty,

By all your vows of love, and that great vow

Which did incorporate and make us one,

That you unfold to me, yourself, your half,

Why you are heavy, and what men tonight

Have had to resort to you – for here have been

Some six or seven, who did hide their faces

Even from darkness.

Within the bond of marriage, tell me, Brutus.

Is it excepted I should know no secrets

That appertain to you? Am I your self

But as it were in sort or limitation?

To keep with you at meals, comfort your bed,

And talk to you sometimes? Dwell I but in the suburbs

Of your good pleasure? If it be no more,

Portia is Brutus' harlot, not his wife.

KING JOHN

King John (1166-1216) is on the throne of England. He is rather a weak King but has a dominating mother, Queen Elinor, who is determined to keep her son on the English throne. Meanwhile, her daughter in law, Constance, is in France and is adamant that her son Arthur, is the legal heir to the English throne. She has the support of France for this claim and France and England are willing to go to war over this.

There are two brothers, Robert Faulconbridge and his half-brother, Philip Faulconbridge (called the Bastard of Faulconbridge) who are arguing over their father's lands and inheritance. King John is very fond of the illegitimate Philip and believes he bears a resemblance to Richard the Lionheart, his great elder brother. He suggests that Philip should rejects his claim to the Falconbridge lands and claim Richard as his father. Queen Elinor also is happy to accept the amiable Philip and he agrees to fight under their colours.

Meanwhile, Austria has joined with France to fight for Prince Arthur's claim. King John arrives in France along with his mother, Queen Elinor. A vicious quarrel breaks out between Constance and Elinor after which Elinor, Arthur's grandmother, tries to persuade Arthur to return with her to England. A battle ensues in France and eventually a truce is agreed by which Elinor's niece, Blanche, is married to King Philip of France's son, Lewis. Constance is furious. She defends her son, Arthur, vehemently. The two countries are now allies for a while until the Pope arrives in France. He is unhappy with the authority of the English church. France decides to retain its' loyalty to Rome and thus breaks off its' alliance with England.

Another battle ensues and King John captures the young Arthur. He persuades Arthur that he will be safe with his grandmother,

Elinor. In reality, he knows the boy is a threat to his position on the throne and orders Hubert to imprison the boy and later kill him.

Hubert, despite actually bringing in evil henchman to carry out the murderous deed of the young Arthur, under King John's orders, cannot bring himself to hurt the young boy and allows him to escape. King John conducts a second coronation for himself. Even though Hubert's conscience allows Arthur to escape, unfortunately the young boy leaps from one of the battlements and is killed on the stones beneath. The nobles react badly to Arthur's death and blame both Hubert and King John for this royal death. Later, due to the intervention of Philip, the bastard of Faulconbridge, Hubert is spared. There is news that the French have invaded England and that Queen Elinor is dead. In anger against King John, many of the English nobles change sides and support the French invasion. It is only when Philip the bastard, takes command of the army, and challenges the French, that affiliations once again change and the English are victorious. The weakened King John, dies and the throne is passed on to his son.

KING JOHN ACT 3 SC 1

(Constance has heard news from Salisbury that France has befriended England. Lewis has married Blanch to secure relations with both countries. Arthur, the rightful heir to the throne is with his mother, Constance. King John is on the throne of England).

<u>Constance:</u>

Gone to be married! Gone to swear a peace!

False blood to false blood join'd! gone to be friends!

Shall Lewis have Blanch, and Blanch those provinces?

It is not so: thou hast misspoke, mis-heard;

Be well advis'd, tell o'er thy tale again:

It cannot be; thou dost but say, 't is so.

I trust, I may not trust thee, for thy word

Is but the vain breath of a common man:

Believe me, I do not believe thee, man:

I have a king's oath to the contrary.

Thou shalt be punish'd for thus frighting me;

For I am sick, and capable of fears;

Oppress'd with wrongs, and therefore full of fears;

A widow, husbandless, subject to fears;

A woman, naturally born to fears;

And though thou now confess thou didst but jest,

With my vex'd spirits I cannot take a truce,

But they will quake and tremble all this day.

What dost thou mean by shaking of thy head?

Why dost thou look so sadly on my son?

What means that hand upon that breast of thine?

Why holds thine eye that lamentable rheum,

Like a proud river peering o'er his bounds?

Be these sad signs confirmers of thy words?

Then speak again; not all thy former tale,

But this one word, whether thy tale be true.

O! If thou teach me to believe this sorrow,

Teach thou this sorrow how to make me die;

And let belief and life encounter so,

As doth the fury of two desperate men,

Which is the very meeting fall, and die. –

Lewis marry Blanch! O boy! Then where art thou?

France friends with England, what becomes of me? –

Fellow be gone; I cannot brook thy sight:

This news hath made thee a most ugly man.

If thou, that bid'st me be content, wert grim,

Ugly, and slanderous to thy mother's womb,

Full of unpleasing blots and sightless stains,

Lame, foolish, crooked, swart, prodigious,

Patch'd with foul moles, and eye-offending marks,

I would not care, I then would be content;

For then I should not love thee; no, nor thou

Become thy great birth, nor deserve a crown.

But thou art fair; and at thy birth, dear boy,

Nature and Fortune join'd to make thee great:

Of Nature's gifts thou may'st with lilies boast,

And with the half-blown rose. But Fortune, O!

She is corrupted, chang'd, and won from thee:

She adulterates hourly with thine Uncle John;

And with her golden hand hath pluck'd on France

To tread down fair respect of sovereignty,

And make his majesty the bawd to theirs.

France is a bawd to Fortune, and King John;

That strumpet Fortune, that usurping John! –

Tell me, thou fellow, is not France forsworn?

Envenom him with words, or get thee gone,

And leave those woes alone, which I alone

Am bound to underbear.

                    I will not go with thee.

I will instruct my sorrows to be proud,

For grief is proud, and makes his owner stoop.

To me, and to the state of my great grief,

Let kings assemble; for my grief's so great,

That no supporter but the huge firm earth

Can hold it up: here I and sorrow sit;

Here is my throne, bid kings come bow to it.

KING JOHN ACT 3 SC 4

(Constance has been separated from Prince Arthur, her son, who is the rightful heir to the throne. King John has usurped the throne of England. She is talking to the Cardinal).

Constance:

Thou art unholy to belie me so.

I am not mad; this hair I tear, is mine;

My name is Constance; I was Geffrey's wife.

Young Arthur is my son, and he is lost!

I am not mad; - I would to Heaven I were,

For then, 'tis like I should forget myself;

O, if I could, what grief should I forget! –

Preach some philosophy to make me mad,

And thou shalt be canonis'd, cardinal;

For, being not mad, but sensible of grief,

My reasonable part produces reason

How I may be deliver'd of these woes,

And teaches me to kill or hang myself:

If I were mad, I should forget my son,

Or madly think a babe of clouts were he.

I am not mad: too well, too well I feel

The different plague of each calamity.

           Bind up my hairs?

Yes, that I will: and wherefore will I do it?

I tore them from their bonds, and cried aloud,

"O, that these hands could so redeem my son,

As they have given these hairs their liberty!'

But now I envy at their liberty,

And will again commit them to their bonds,

Because my poor child is a prisoner -

And, father cardinal, I have heard you say,

That we shall see and know our friends in heaven.

If that be true, I shall see my boy again;

For, since the birth of Cain, the first male child,

To him that did but yesterday suspire,

There was not such a gracious creature born.

But now will canker sorrow eat my bud,

And chase the native beauty from his cheek,

And he will look as hollow as a ghost,

As dim and meagre as an ague's fit,

And so he'll die; and rising so again,

When I shall meet him in the court of heaven,

I shall not know him; therefore, never, never

Must I behold my pretty Arthur more.

HENRY IV PART I

Henry IV succeeds Richard III. Harry Percy otherwise known as Hotspur, is the King's most heroic soldier and has been quelling rebellions in Wales and Scotland. He has taken many prisoners. The king's own son, Prince Hal is irresponsible and has not grown up, preferring to spend his time in taverns with his friends. Mistress Quickly is the owner of the tavern which Prince Hal frequents. One of his great companions is John Falstaff and they spend much of their time playing pranks on others. The scenes between Falstaff and the young prince provide the comic subplot of the play. Hotspur becomes stronger and stronger, surrounded by his father and uncle. The King is concerned about his increasing power. When the King rebukes Hotspur over his dealings with the Scottish prisoners and the Mortimer family, who have some claim to the throne, Hotspur takes offence and suggests to his family that they should join forces with the Welsh and Scottish in a bid for the throne. Lady Percy, Hotspur's wife, is Mortimer's sister. He decides to send her away for her own safety. He will not divulge his plans to her, despite their close and loving relationship. Mistress Quickly hears news of the uprising and warns Prince Hal of the dangers of Percy, Douglas, Mortimer and Owen Glendower, reminding him of his own claim to his father's throne. Prince Hal returns to the King and in a long speech tells him that he is his son and that he has what it takes to be King. He aims to prove it to him. King Henry, convinced by his son's change of attitude, puts him in charge of his army.

Hotspur, full of fighting spirit, learns that his own allies are not ready and have not been able to raise their armies sufficiently. King Henry offers his enemies a chance to be pardoned but Hotspur's uncle does not relay the message. Falstaff has joined the army of his best friend, Hal, but unfortunately many of his motley crew do not survive the battle. Falstaff, essentially a coward and not fit for battle, feigns his death and miraculously survives the battle. Prince Hal eventually seeks out Hotspur and kills him. The mischievous Falstaff suggests it was he that had killed Hotspur and asks for a title. Despite this lie, Prince Hal bestows a title on his dear friend. The prince now has to deal with the other traitors – Douglas, Mortimer, Glendower and Lord Percy Senior.

(Kate, Lady Percy, is beseeching her husband, Hotspur, to share his concerns with her. Lord Percy is planning to leave Warkworth castle within two hours).

Lady Percy:

O, my good lord! Why are you thus alone?

For what offence have I this fortnight been

A banish'd woman from my Harry's bed?

Tell me, sweet lord, what is't that takes from thee

Thy stomach, pleasure, and thy golden sleep?

Why dost thou bend thine eyes upon the earth,

And start so often when thou sit'st alone?

Why hast thou lost the fresh blood in thy cheeks,

And given my treasures, and my rights of thee,

To thick-eyed 'musing, and curst melancholy?

In thy faint slumbers I by thee hath watch'd,

And heard thee murmur tales of iron wars,

Speak terms of manage to thy bouncing steed,

Cry, "Courage! – to the field!" And thou hast talked

Of sallies, and retires; of trenches, tents,

Of palisades, frontiers, parapets,

Of basilisks, of cannon, culverin.

Of prisoners' ransom, and of soldiers slain.

And all the currents of a heady fight.

Thy spirit within thee hath been so at war,

And thus hath so bestirred thee in thy sleep,

That beads of sweat have stood upon thy brow,

Like bubbles in a late-disturbed stream;

And in thy face strange motions have appeared,

Such as we see when men restrain their breath

On some great sudden hest. O! what portents are these?

Some heavy business hath my lord in hand,

And I must know it, else he loves me not.

Come, come, you paraquito, answer me

Directly unto this question that I ask.

In faith, I'll break thy little finger, Harry,

And if thou wilt not tell me all things true.

Do you not love me? Do you not, indeed?

Well, do not then; for since you love me not,

I will not love myself. Do you not love me?

Nay, tell me, if you speak in jest, or no?

OTHELLO

Othello is a tragedy about a black General, named Othello who is overcome with jealousy. The play is set in Venice. Iago, a soldier, hates Othello as he has been overlooked for promotion as lieutenant and is intent on revenge. Iago and Roderigo, who is in love with Desdemona, plan to accuse Othello's wife, Desdemona, of infidelity. The marriage between Othello and Desdemona has been conducted in secret and her father, Brabantio, is not happy, especially when Desdemona chooses her husband over her father. The Turks are planning an attack on Cyprus and there are plans to send Othello to defend the island. Othello asks Iago to protect Desdemona whilst he sails on ahead. Iago wants to destroy Othello's marriage and take revenge on Michael Cassio. Desdemona, Iago, his wife, Emilia, and Michael Cassio set sail later for Cyprus. Iago plans to accuse Cassio of being Desdemona's lover. Iago succeeds in getting Cassio drunk, picks a fight with him and makes Othello believe it is all Cassio's fault. Iago suggests Cassio use Desdemona's loyalty and friendship to get back into favor with Othello. Iago plants the seed of infidelity in Othello's mind. He then asks his wife, Emilia, to steal a specially embroidered handkerchief which was a gift from Othello to Desdemona. He plants this handkerchief in Cassio's lodgings as 'proof' that Desdemona has been with him. Othello questions Desdemona on the whereabouts of her handkerchief, saying that if she has lost it, she has lost his love! Othello interrogates her maid, Emilia, who will not betray her mistress. Desdemona is completely innocent and does not understand what has happened. Meanwhile, Roderigo and Iago attempt to kill Cassio. Othello is so enraged that he kills Desdemona. Emilia reveals that Othello has killed his wife and that Iago had stolen the handkerchief. Cassio appears, having survived the attempted assassination. Othello apologizes and kills himself. Cassio is declared the new governor of Cyprus and Iago will be suitably punished.

OTHELLO ACT 1, SC. 3

(Desdemona is speaking her father and the Duke of Venice. She is trying to explain the difference between the love of a daughter to her father and that of a wife to her husband).

Desdemona:

My noble father,

I do perceive here a divided duty:

To you I am bound for life and education;

My life and education both do learn me

How to respect you; you are the lord of duty;

I am hitherto your daughter: but here's my husband,

And so much duty as my mother show'd

To you, preferring you before her father,

So much I challenge that I may profess

Due to the Moor my lord.

Nor I; I would not there reside,

To put my father in impatient thoughts

By being in his eye. Most gracious duke,

To my unfolding lend your prosperous ear;

And let me find a charter in your voice,

To assist my simpleness.

That I did love the Moor to live with him,

My downright violence and storm of fortunes

May trumpet to the world: my heart's subdued

Even to the very quality of my lord:

I saw Othello's visage in his mind,

And to his honour and his valiant parts

Did I my soul and fortunes consecrate.

So that, dear lords, if I be left behind,

A moth of peace, and he go to the war.

The rites for which I love him are bereft me,

And I a heavy interim shall support

By his dear absence. Let me go with him.

OTHELLO ACT 3, SC 3

(Desdemona tries to convince Othello that Cassio is a good man. Cassio is at present out of favour with Othello).

<u>Desdemona:</u>

How now, my lord!

I have been talking with a suitor here,

A man that languishes in your displeasure.

Why, your lieutenant, Cassio. Good my lord,

If I have any grace or power to move you,

His present reconciliation take;

For if he be not one that truly loves you,

That errs in ignorance and not in cunning,

I have no judgment in an honest face:

I prithee, call him back.

Ay, sooth; so humbled

That he hath left part of his grief with me,

To suffer with him. Good love, call him back.

But shall't be shortly?

Shall't be to-night at supper?

To-morrow dinner, then?

Why, then, to-morrow night; or Tuesday morn;

On Tuesday noon, or night; on Wednesday morn:

I prithee, name the time, but let it not

Exceed three days: in faith, he's penitent;

And yet his trespass, in our common reason-

Save that, they say, the wars must make examples

Out of their best – is not almost a fault

To incur a private check. When shall he come?

Tell me, Othello: I wonder in my soul,

What you would ask me, that I should deny,

Or stand so mammering on. What! Michael Cassio,

That came a-wooing with you, and so many a time,

When I have spoke of you dispraisingly,

Hath ta'en your part; to have so much to do

To bring him in! Trust me, I could do much –

Prithee, no more: let him come when he will;

I will deny thee nothing.

You will deny me nothing. Why, this is not a boon;

'T is as I should entreat you wear your gloves,

Or feed on nourishing dishes, or keep you warm,

Or sue to you to do a peculiar profit

To your own person: nay when I have a suit

Wherein I mean to touch your love indeed,

It shall be full of poise and difficult weight,

And fearful to be granted. Farewell, my lord.

OTHELLO ACT 4, SC 3

(Othello is in a jealous rage believing his wife, Desdemona, has been unfaithful to him. He has bid his wife to go to bed immediately. Emilia, her waiting woman is with Desdemona, trying to comfort her).

Desdemona:

He says he will return incontinent:

He hath commanded me to go to bed

And bid me to dismiss you.

It was his bidding: therefore, good Emilia,

Give me my nightly wearing, and adieu:

We must not now displease him.

(She asks Emilia to help her undress & take down her hair).

Prithee, unpin me, - have grace and favour in them.

All's one. Good faith, how foolish are our minds!

If I do die before thee prithee, shroud me

In one of those same sheets.

My mother had a maid call'd Barbara:

She was in love, and he she loved proved mad

And did forsake her: she had a song of 'willow';

An old thing 'twas, but it express'd her fortune,

And she died singing it: that song to-night

Will not go from my mind; I have much to do,

But to go hang my head all at one side,

And sing it like poor Barbara. Prithee, dispatch.

No, unpin me here.

(Desdemona sings in a melancholy fashion, feeling something untoward is about to happen).

The poor soul sat sighing by a sycamore tree,

Sing all a green willow:

Her hand on her bosom, her head on her knee,

Sing willow, willow, willow:

The fresh streams ran by her, and murmur'd her moans;

Sing willow, willow, willow;

Her salt tears fell from her, and soften'd the stones;

(She asks Emilia to put her clothes away & lay out the bedsheets).

Lay be these: -

(singing) Sing, willow, willow, willow;

Prithee, hie thee, he'll come anon: -

(singing)

Sing all a green willow must be my garland.

Let nobody blame him; his scorn I approve,-

Nay, that's not next. – Hark! Who is't that knocks?

(singing)

I call'd my love false love; but what said he then?

Sing willow, willow, willow:

If I court moe women, you'll couch with moe men!

So, get thee gone; good night. Mine eyes do itch;

Doth that bode weeping?

I have heard it said so. O, these men, these men!

Dost thou in conscience think, - tell me, Emilia, -

That there be women do abuse their husbands

In such gross kind?

Wouldst thou do such a deed for all the world?

No, by this heavenly light!

Wouldst thou do such a deed for all the world?

In troth, I think thou wouldst not.

I do not think there is any such woman.

Good night, good night: heaven me such uses send,

Not to pick bad from bad, but by bad mend!

HAMLET

Hamlet is a revenge tragedy. The play is set in Denmark at the
Castle of Elsinore. The play begins with the ghost of the late King
of Denmark walking the battlements, as if to warn his citizens of
some imminent danger. There is a threat of war between
neighbouring Norway. Hamlet's friend, Horatio, sees the ghost
and tells his best friend, Hamlet. Gertrude, the Queen, has
married her husband's brother, Claudius, in less than two months
of her husband's death. Hamlet is beside himself with grief and
outrage. Polonius, the Lord Chamberlain, has a son, Laertes, and
a beautiful daughter, Ophelia, whom Hamlet has been courting.
Hamlet and Horatio visit the battlements with a view to seeing the
ghost again. The ghost appears again and Hamlet learns that his
father's death was most unnatural. He was poisoned by his own
brother, Claudius. From this point on, Hamlet is distraught and
determined for revenge. The court begin to worry about Hamlet's
behaviour. Hamlet is rough in his treatment of Ophelia and kills
her father, Polonius, for spying. Hamlet is also physically
aggressive towards his mother, Gertrude. A group of travelling
players visit the castle and Hamlet asks them to perform a play
'The Murder of Gonzago', which includes the poisoning of a King.
Hamlet wants to see if his uncle reacts guiltily. Claudius fully
obliges and it is clear to Hamlet that he is indeed guilty. Claudius's
response to this is to remove Hamlet from Denmark. He asks
Rosencrantz and Guildenstern to assist him in this task and to
monitor Hamlet's movements. After Hamlet kills Polonius, he has
a good excuse to send him to England. On the way there, Hamlet
encounters the Prince of Norway. Meanwhile, the grief of losing
her father and being spurned by Hamlet is too much for Ophelia
and she loses her mind and shortly after takes her own life. On
returning to England, Hamlet discovers on passing the graveyard
that Ophelia is now dead. Laertes and Hamlet argue. Claudius
directs Laertes to kill Hamlet by challenge him to a duel with a
poisoned a rapier. There is also a poisoned chalice, but Hamlet,

preoccupied with the duel does not drink it and the Queen takes sip from the chalice instead. The poisoned rapier changes hands and Laertes is poisoned. On realising this, Hamlet seizes the sword and stabs the King. He then drinks the poisoned wine from the chalice himself. In Hamlet's dying speech, he hands his role over to Horatio, whilst also stating his wishes are for the Prince of Norway to rule Denmark.

HAMLET ACT 4, SC 5

(Ophelia, distraught by the loss of her father and Hamlet's abusive treatment of her, has lost her mind. She is carrying a bunch of flowers and herbs. These herbs have symbolic significance. The verses in italics are sung).

Ophelia:

Where is the beauteous majesty of Denmark?

(song)

'How should I your true Love Know,

From another one?

By his cockle hat and staff

And his sandal shoon'

(spoken)

They say the owl was the baker's daughter. Lord we know what we are but not what we may be. God be at your table!

(song)

'Tomorrow is Saint Valentine's Day

All in the morning betime

And I a maid at your window

To be your valentine.

'Then up he rose and donn'd his clothes

And dupp'd the chamber door;

Let in the maid, that out the maid

Never departed more'

(spoken)

I'll make an end on't.

(*song*)

'By Gis and by Saint Charity,

Alack and fie for shame!

Young men will do't, if they come to't;

By cock, they are to blame'

Quoth she "before you tumbled me,

You promised me to wed."

"So would I 'a done, by yonder sun,

And thou hast not come to my bed."

(spoken)

I hope all will be well. We must be patient; but I cannot choose but weep to think they would lay him in the cold ground.

(*Ophelia hands out the flowers and herbs to the Queen Gertrude and the King Claudius*)

There's rosemary, that for remembrance; pray you, love, remember. And there's pansies, that's for thoughts. There's fennel for you, and columbines. There rue for you, and here's some fore me.

We may call it herb of grace on Sundays. O, you must wear your rue with a difference. There's a daisy. I would give you some violets, but they withered all when my father died. They say a' made a good end.

(*song*)

'He is dead and gone lady

He is dead and gone

By his head a grass green turf

At his head a stone'

'They bore him barefaced on the bier;

And in his grave rained many a tear'.

(*Spoken line*)

Fare you well. My dove!

'And will 'a not come again?

And will 'a not come again?'

(*spoken*)

He never will come again.

'His beard was white as snow,

All flaxen was his poll;

He is gone, he is gone,

And we cast away moan'.

God 'a mercy on his soul.

And of all Christian souls, I pray God. God b'ye you.

Come, my coach! Good night, ladies; good night, sweet ladies, good night, goodnight.

ROMEO AND JULIET

Believed to have been written between 1591 and 1595,
Romeo and Juliet is a tragedy which is set in Verona, Italy. There
is a feud between two houses: the house of Capulet and the
house of Montague. Romeo does not join in the street fighting
between the two rival gangs. He is sick for the unrequited love of a
young girl named Rosaline. Lord Capulet hosts a masked ball. He
is keen for Paris to court his young daughter, Juliet. Romeo is
dared by his friend, Benvolio, along with Mercutio, to gatecrash
this ball. Romeo is easily persuaded as he believes that Rosaline
will be there. On seeing Juliet, Romeo quickly forgets Rosaline.
The fiery Capulet, Tybalt overhears Romeo asking after Juliet and
realizes that he is a Montague. Romeo manages to dance with
Juliet and steal a kiss from her. Juliet has now fallen in love with
Romeo. That night, Romeo climbs the wall of the Capulet's house
and finds Juliet on her balcony. They profess their love for each
other and Romeo promises to find a way in which they can be
married. Juliet arranges to send her beloved nurse the next
morning at nine o'clock to finalize the arrangements. Romeo
meets with the Friar who agrees to conduct a secret marriage. He
hopes that marriage between two warring households may resolve
matters. Tybalt has sent Romeo a letter challenging him to a duel.
Romeo does not want to fight with Tybalt as he knows he is
Juliet's cousin. Romeo and Juliet are secretly married that
afternoon by Friar Laurence. The duel takes place and Mercutio is
killed by Tybalt and despite Romeo's reluctance to fight, he is
enraged at Mercutio's death and kills Tybalt. Romeo is banished
and must leave Verona by the next morning and never return.
Meanwhile, Juliet is waiting for Romeo to enjoy their wedding
night. Her joy turns to sorrow when she learns from her nurse that
Tybalt has been slain. Romeo spends the night with his new bride
before leaving at dawn. That morning, Lady Capulet informs Juliet
that she is to marry Paris. Juliet, in desperation, begs the Friar to
help her. He offers her a potion which will feign the appearance of
death. When she is laid in the vault, Romeo will be able to come
and be reunited with her. Unfortunately, Romeo does not receive
the letter and believes that Juliet is dead. Romeo buys poison so
that he can lie alongside his beloved Juliet. Paris arrives at the
tomb to mourn Juliet and sees Romeo. A duel ensues. Paris is

killed. Romeo takes Juliet in his arms and drinks the poison. He kisses Juliet one last time. Juliet awakes to find Romeo dead. She then kills herself with a dagger no longer wishing to live. The violent feud between the two warring families is ended.

ROMEO & JULIET ACT 2 SC 2

(The Balcony scene. Juliet has recently met Romeo at a masked ball and fallen in love with him. Little does she know that Romeo has stolen into the grounds of the Capulet's house and is listening to her speaking romantically about him).

<u>Juliet:</u>

O Romeo, Romeo, wherefore art thou Romeo?

Deny thy father and refuse thy name,

Or if thou wilt not, be but sworn my love,

And I'll no longer be a Capulet.

'Tis but thy name that is my enemy.

Thou art thyself, though not a Montague.

What's Montague? It is nor hand, nor foot,

Nor arm, nor face, nor any other part

Belonging to a man. O, be some other name!

What's in a name? That which we call a rose

By any other word would smell as sweet.

So Romeo would, were he not Romeo called,

Retain that dear perfection which he owes

Without that title. Romeo, doff thy name,

And for thy name – which is no part of thee –

Take all myself.

(Juliet notices a stranger lurking in the dark)

What man art thou that thus bescreen'd in night

So stumblest on my counsel?

(Juliet suddenly realizes that it is Romeo)

Art thou not Romeo and a Montague?

How camest thou hither, tell me, and wherefore?

The orchard walls are high and hard to climb,

And the place death, considering who thou art,

If any of my kinsmen find thee here.

(Juliet is now embarrassed that Romeo has heard her speaking romantically about him)

Thou knowest the mask of night is on my face,

Else would a maiden blush bepaint my cheek

For that which thou hast heard me speak tonight.

Fain would I dwell on form fain, fain deny

What I have spoke; but farewell, compliment.

Dost thou love me? I know thou wilt say "Ay,"

And I will take thy word. Yet if thou swear'st

Thou mayst prove false. At lovers' perjuries,

They say, Jove laughs. O gentle Romeo,

If thou dost love, pronounce it faithfully;

Or if thou think'st I am too quickly won,

I'll frown, and be perverse, and say thee nay,

So thou wilt woo; but else, not for the world.

In truth, fair Montague, I am too fond,

And therefore, thou mayst think my 'haviour light.

But trust me, gentleman, I'll prove more true

Than those that have more cunning to be strange.

I would have been more strange, I must confess,

But that thou overheard'st, 'ere I was ware,

My true-love passion. Therefore, pardon me,

And not impute this yielding to light love,

Which the dark night hath so discovered.

ROMEO & JULIET ACT 3, SC 2

(Juliet's excitement rapidly turns to sorrow. It is to be her wedding night but when the nurse enters, she has sad news regarding her cousin, Tybalt).

<u>Juliet:</u>

Gallop apace, you fiery-footed steeds,

Towards Phoebus' lodging! Such a waggoner

As Phaeton would whip you to the West

And bring in cloudy night immediately.

Spread thy close curtain, love-performing night,

That runaway's eyes may wink, and Romeo

Leap to these arms untalked of and unseen.

Lovers can see to do their amorous rites

By their own beauties; or, if love be blind,

It best agrees with night. Come, civil night,

Thou sober-suited matron, all in black,

And learn me how to lose a winning match,

Played for a pair of stainless maidenhoods.

Hood my unmanned blood, bating in my cheeks,

With thy black mantle till strange love grow bold,

Think true love acted simple modesty.

Come, night. Come, Romeo. Come, thou day in night;

For thou wilt lie upon the wings of night

Whiter than new snow upon a raven's back.

Come, gentle night. Come, loving, black-browed night.

Give me my Romeo. And when I shall die,

Take him and cut him out in little stars,

And he will make the face of heaven so fine

That all the world will be in love with night

And pay no worship to the garish sun.

O I have bought the mansion of a love,

But not possessed it; and though I am sold,

Not yet enjoyed. So tedious is this day

As is the night before some festival

To an impatient child that hath new robes

And may not wear them.

O here comes my Nurse,

And she brings news; and every tongue that speaks

But Romeo's name speaks heavenly eloquence.

Now, Nurse, what news?

(The nurse enters and tells Juliet that Tybalt has been slain and that Romeo is banished)

O Tybalt, Tybalt, the best friend I had!

O God! Did Romeo's hand shed Tybalt's blood?

Shall I speak ill of him that is my husband?

Ah, poor my lord, what tongue shall smooth thy name

When I, thy three-hours wife, have mangled it?

But wherefore, villain, didst thou kill my cousin?

That villain cousin would have killed my husband.

Back, foolish tears, back to your native spring!

Your tributary drops belong to woe,

Which you, mistaking, offer up to joy.

My husband lives, that Tybalt would have slain;

And Tybalt's dead, that would have slain my husband.

All this is comfort. Wherefore weep I then?

Some word there was, worser than Tybalt's death,

That murdered me. I would forget it fain.

But O, it presses to my memory

Like damned guilty deeds to sinners' minds!

'Tybalt is dead, and Romeo - banished.'

That 'banished', that one word 'banished',

Hath slain ten thousand Tybalts. Tybalt's death

Was woe enough, if it had ended there;

Or, if sour woe delights in fellowship

And needly will be ranked with other griefs,

Why followed not, when she said "Tybalt's dead',

Thy father, or thy mother, nay, or both,

Which modern lamentation might have moved?

But with a rearward following Tybalt's death,

'Romeo is banished' - to speak that word

Is father, mother, Tybalt, Romeo, Juliet,

All slain, all dead. 'Romeo is banished' -

There is no end, no limit, measure, bound,

In that word's death. No words can that woe sound.

Where is my father and my mother, Nurse?

Take up those cords. Poor ropes, you are beguiled,

Both you and I, for Romeo is exiled.

ROMEO & JULIET ACT 4, SC 3

(The potion scene. Juliet is distraught by the fact that Romeo has been banished. She decides to take a potion to feign her death in the hope that she can be later reunited with Romeo).

Juliet:

Farewell! God knows when we shall meet again.

I have a faint cold fear thrills through my veins

That almost freezes up the heat of life:

I'll call them back again to comfort me.

Nurse! – What should she do here?

My dismal scene I needs must act alone.

Come vial.

What if this mixture do not work at all?

Shall I be married then tomorrow morning?

No, no, this shall forbid it; lie thou there.

(She lays down the dagger)

What if it be a poison which the Friar

Subtly hath ministered to have me dead,

Lest in this marriage he should be dishonoured,

Because he married me before to Romeo?

I fear it is, and yet methinks it should not,

For he hath still been tried a holy man.

How, if, when I am laid into the tomb,

I wake before the time that Romeo

Come to redeem me? There's a fearful point!

Shall I not then be stifled in the vault,

To whose foul mouth no healthsome air breathes in,

And there die strangled ere my Romeo comes?

Or if I live, is it not very like

The horrible conceit of death and night,

Together with the terror of the place –

As in a vault, an ancient receptacle,

Where for this many hundred years the bones

Of all my buried ancestors are packed,

Where bloody Tybalt, yet but green in earth,

Lies fest'ring in his shroud, where, as they say,

At some hours in the night spirits resort –

Alack, alack, is it not like that I,

So early waking – what with loathsome smells,

And shrieks like mandrakes' torn out of the earth,

That living mortals hearing them run mad –

O, if I wake, shall I not be distraught,

Environed with all these hideous fears,

And madly play with my forefathers' joints,

And pluck the mangled Tybalt from his shroud,

And in this rage, with some great kinsman's bone,

As with a club, dash out my desp'rate brains?

O look! Methinks I see my cousin's ghost

Seeking out Romeo that did spit his body

Upon a rapier's point. Stay, Tybalt, stay!

Romeo, Romeo, Romeo! Here's drink – I drink to thee.

KING LEAR

King Lear is a tragedy. The 80 yr old King is becoming old and a little senile. It is time for him to relinquish his kingdom and share it between his three daughters, Goneril, Regan and Cordelia. He states, in his foolishness, that whichever daughter proves to love him best will inherit most of his kingdom. As Cordelia is less sycophantic than her elder sisters, Lear childishly rejects his youngest daughter who had once been his favourite. Cordelia marries the King of France and leaves her two unscrupulous sisters to take care of their father. King Lear's prime minister, Gloucester is also betrayed by his son, Edmund, and his other faithful son, Edgar, is forced to go into hiding. The two sisters plot against their father and the king and his fool end up in the wilderness together, battling the elements. Gloucester, the prime minister, is blinded. The whole kingdom and the royal family collapse. The faithful Kent finds Lear and tries to protect him. It seems that his daughters do not care for him. In fact, Regan has been plotting against his life. Both daughters expel Lear from their homes. Lear manages to get to France where the French army, along with Cordelia, come to his rescue. By this time, Lear has gone quite mad. He makes his peace with the gentle Cordelia. There is a battle between the French and the English and the French are defeated. Lear and Cordelia are captured. Greedy for position, Goneril poisons her own sister, Regan. The evil Edmund is pronounced a traitor and the loyal Edgar wins the battle. Edgar orders Cordelia to be released but alas, it is too late. She has already been hanged. Lear enters with his daughter's dead body in his arms. King Lear dies of a broken heart.

KING LEAR ACT 1, SC 4

(Goneril is speaking to Oswald about her father's foolish behaviour. She wants Oswald to obey her commands in future).

Goneril:

Did my father strike my gentleman for chiding of his fool?

By day and night he wrongs me: every hour

He flashes into one gross crime or other,

That sets us all at odds: I'll not endure it.

His knight's grow riotous, and himself upbraids us

On every trifle. – When he returns from hunting,

I will not speak with him; say, I am sick:

If you come slack of former services,

You shall do well: the fault of it I'll answer.

Put on what weary negligence you please.

You and your fellows: I'd have it come to question:

If he distaste it, let him to my sister,

Whose mind and mine, I know, in that are one,

Not to be over-rul'd. Idle old man,

That still would manage those authorities

That he hath given away! – Now, by my life,

Old fools are babes again; and must be us'd

With checks, as flatteries, when they are seen abus'd.

Remember what I have said.

And let his knights have colder looks among you;

What grows of it, no matter; advise your fellows so:

I would breed from hence occasions, and I shall,

That I may speak: - I'll write straight to my sister,

To hold my course. – Prepare for dinner.

KING LEAR ACT 2, SC 4

(Reagan is trying to convince her father, King Lear, to return to her sister, Goneril. Lear refuses as he feels he has been betrayed by Goneril. Shortly after their conversation, Goneril arrives)

<u>Reagan:</u>

I am glad to see your highness.

I pray you, sir, take patience. I have hope

You less know how to value her desert,

Than she to scant her duty.

I cannot think my sister in the least

Would fail her obligation: If, sir, perchance,

She has restrained the riots of your followers,

'Tis on such ground, and to such wholesome end,

As clears her from all blame.

O, sir! You are old;

Nature in you stands on the very verge

Of her confine: You should be rul'd and led

By some discretion that discerns your state

Better than you yourself. Therefore, I pray you,

That to our sister you do make return;

Say, you have wrong'd her, sir.

Good sir, no more: These are unsightly tricks.

Return you to my sister.

O the blest gods! So will you wish on me,

When the rash mood is on.

Good sir, to the purpose.

What trumpet's that?

I know't, my sister's; this approves her letter,

That she would soon be here. Is your lady come?

(Goneril enters)

I pray you father, being weak, seem so.

If, till the expiration of your month,

You will return and sojourn with my sister,

Dismissing half your train, come then to me:

I am now from home and out of that provision

Which shall be needful for your entertainment.

ABOUT THE AUTHOR

Kim Gilbert trained as a professional actress at the Guildford School of Acting, Guildhall School of Music and Drama and at the Open University. She has been acting, teaching and directing plays and musical productions for more than 35 years. She has experience in a wide range of theatre, TV and voiceover work. She has a First-class Honours degree in English and has taught English and Drama in many top schools in the country. Kim has examined for Lamda for a number of years and also acted as an adjudicator. She has been running Dramatic Arts Studio for 11yrs, a private drama studio which specialises in developing excellence in all forms of performance and communication.

Other Books by the same author:

<u>Shakespeare Scenes</u>

Monologues for young female actors

Duologues for female actors

Monologues for young male actors

<u>Chekhov Scenes</u>

Monologues & Duologues for women

Monologues for Male Actors

<u>Scenes from Oscar Wilde</u>

Monologues & duologues for female actors

Monologues for male actors

Duologues for male & female actors

<u>Classical Scenes</u>

Monologues for female actors

Available from Amazon Bookstore

"Thanks for reading! If you enjoyed this book or found it useful, I'd be very grateful if you'd post a short review on Amazon. Your support really does make a difference and I read all the reviews personally so I can get your feedback and make this book even better.

Thankyou for your support!"

Shakespeare Scenes

Printed in Great Britain
by Amazon